Published by Aperitifs Publishing Company
Santa Rosa, California
707-523-1611
johncburton@msn.com

ISBN: 978-1-7324530-5-0
Library of Congress Control Number: 2023903377

Written by Tim Higgins
Original manuscript and all rights to this publication purchased by John C. Burton September 2022

Copyright: September 2022
John C. Burton

Printed in the United States of America

All rights reserved. No part of this book may be reproduced or transformed in any form or by any means, electronic or mechanical, including photocopying, recording or by any information storage and/or retrieval system without permission in writing from the author or publisher.

Every attempt has been made to provide accurate information on the following subjects.

johncburton@msn.com
707-523-1611

ACKNOWLEDGMENTS

MANY PEOPLE HELPED WITH THE PRODUCTION OF THIS BOOK. BELOW IS A LIST OF THE SOURCES AND PEOPLE WHO MADE THIS BOOK POSSIBLE.

DEREK ABRAMS, SANTA MARIA, CA.
MARK ACCARDI, LOS OSOS, CA.
DAVID BETHMAN, HAMILTON, MONT. (Washington bottles))
WARREN BORTON, MIDVALE, UT. (Wyoming bottles)
DAN BROWN, PETALUMA, CA.
KEN EDWARD, SUTTER CREEK, CA.
WARREN FRIEDRICH, GRASS VALLEY, CA.
JIM HAGENBUCH, EAST GREENVILLE, PA. (Glassworks Auctions)
RICK HALL, SAN DIEGO, CA.
BILL HAM, LAKEPORT, CA.
BRENT HENNINGSEN, SAN DIEGO, CAL.
CHARLES HOLT, HERALD, CA.
STEVE HUBBELL, GIG HARBOR, WASH.
DONALD KING, BENICIA, CA.
ANDREW KOUTSOUKOS, SAN RAFAEL, CA.
LOU LAMBERT, GRATON, CA.
RICK LINDGREN, MARTINEZ, CA.
JON LAWSON, SAN DIEGO, CA.
MARTIN LUDTKE, ARCATA, CA.
VINCE MADRUGA, GILROY, CA.
DALE MLASKO, MEDFORD, ORE.
IVAN OAKESON, SALT LAKE CITY, UT. (Utah bottles)
JOHN O'NEIL, BELMONT, CA.
PEACHRIDGE GLASS (web site)
RICK PISANO, SAN JOSE CA.
GLEN PREBLE, LAKEWOOD, COLO. (Colorado bottles)
LANE PUCKETT, VIRGINIA CITY, NEV.
TOM QUINN, BENICIA, CA.
ROY ROBERTS, INDEPENDENCE, MO.
KEN SALAZAR, SAN FRANCISCO, CA. (the late)
JOHN SCHROYER, REDWOOD CITY, CA.
RICK SIMI, DOWNIEVILLE, CA. (the late)
RICHARD SIRI, SANTA ROSA, CA.
ANTHONY TAYLOR, BROWNSVILLE, CA.
BOB VOEGTLY, TRACY, CA.
WESTERN BOTTLE NEWS, (web site)
JEFF WICHMAN, SACRAMENTO, CA. (American Bottle Auctions)

GLASSWORKS AUCTIONS AND AMERICAN BOTTLE AUCTION SUPPLIED MOST OF THE AUCTION PRICING USED IN THIS BOOK. AMERICAN BOTTLE ALSO HELPED TO FILL IN GAPS WITH MANY OF THE PHOTOS USED HERE. A SPECIAL THANKS TO THEM.

THE OLD BOTTLEMAN
FEBRUARY, 2020

INTRODUCTION

THIS BOOK CONTAINS MANY EARLY WESTERN DRUG AND MEDICINE BOTTLES. IT IS ARRANGED BY STYLE OF THE BOTTLE AND WHAT IT PROBABLY CONTAINED. THERE IS AN INDEX IN THE BACK OF THE LISTINGS THAT IS CROSS REFERENCED, TO HELP FIND THE BOTTLE YOU MAY BE LOOKING FOR.

CONTENTS

CITRATE OF MAGNESIA	1
COSMETIC, SKIN LOTION TYPES	26
EXTRACT STYLE	35
FLORIDA WATER, TOILET WATER	40
JAMAICA GINGER	56
PATENT MEDICINE	65
POT LIDS and OINTMENT POTS	127
SARSAPARILLA	131
EARLY CALIFORNIA DRUG and APOTHECARY	137
EARLY OREGON DRUG and APOTHECARY	152
EARLY NEVADA DRUG and APORHECARY	155
INDEX	

A FEW WORDS ABOUT VALUE. THE PRICES SHOWN IN THE LISTING ARE ACTUAL SELLING PRICES AT AUCTION. BUYER PREMIUMS ARE NOT INCLUDED IN THE PRICE. THE YEAR SOLD FOLLOWS THE PRICE. SOME OF THESE ARE OUT OF DATE, AS THEY HAVE NOT BEEN BROUGHT TO AUCTION IN MANY YEARS. THESE MAY NOT BE RELEVANT IN TODAYS MARKET, BUT I INCLUDED THEM ANYWAY, TO GIVE THE COLLECTOR AN IDEA WHAT HIS ITEM MAY BE WORTH. SOME CATAGORIES HAVE GONE DOWN IN VALUE AND OTHER HAVE GREATLY APPRECIATED OVER THE YEARS. WESTER BLOWN BOTTLES WITH APPLIED TOPS HAVE GONE UP THE MOST. SOME OF THE BOTTLES IN THIS LISTING ARE SO RARE THEY HAVE NOT CHANGED HANDS IN AN AUCTION.

RARITY

THE FOLLOWING SCALE WAS PUT TOGETHER BY MANY PROMINENT AND LONG TIME DIGGERS AND COLLECTORS OF WESTERN MEDICINE BOTTLES. PLEASE KEEP IN MIND THAT SOME MAY BE UNACCOUNTED FOR AS THERE ARE STILL A FEW OLD TIME COLLECTIONS THAT ARE STILL IN THE CLOSET AND UNKOWN.

EXTREMLY RARE	LESS THAN 10 KNOWN
RARE	10-25 KNOWN
SCARCE	25-35 KNOWN
COMMON	MORE THAN 35

CONDITION, COLOR, AND CRUDITY ALL EFFECT VALUE OF ANY BOTTLE. THE STYLE OF TOP USED ALSO CAN GREATLY CHANGE THE VALUE. WESTERN BLOWN BOTTLES WITH APPLIED TOPS ARE MUCH MORE DESIRABLE THAN THE SAME BOTTLE BLOWN IN EASTERN GLASS HOUSES. COLOR IS ANOTHER FACTOR IN A BOTTLES VALUE. FOR EXAMPLE AN E. FRESE JAMIACA GINGER IN AQUA MAY BE SCARCE, BUT IN GREEN OR BLUE IT IS EX. RARE. POLISHING OR TUMBLING A BOTTLE CAN ALSO EFFECT THE BOTTLES VALUE. SOME COLLECTORS PREFER AN UNALTERED BOTTLE, BUT IN MY EXPERIENCE, CLEANING A MEDICINE TYPE BOTTLE USUALLY INHANCES ITS VALUE. CONTACT WITH SOME SOILS CAUSE STAINING TO THE GLASS AND POLISHING CAN REMOVE IT IN MOST CASES.

TERMINOLOGY

Front: EMBOSSING ON THE FRONT OF BOTTLE, USUALLY LISTED FIRST
Side: EMBOSSING ON THE SIDE OF BOTTLE
Re: EMBOSSING ON THE BACK OF BOTTLE
Base: EMBOSSING ON THE BOTTOM OF BOTTLE

/ FOLLOWING A WORD DENOTES A NEW LINE OF EMBOSSING
A.T.-- APPLIED TOP
T.T.-- TOOLED TOP
S.B.-- SMOOTH BASE
I.P.-- IRON PONTIL
O.P.-- OPEN PONTIL

ANY MEASUREMENTS ARE FOR THE HEIGHT OF THE BOTTLE EXCEPT FOR THE POT LIDS, THAN IT IS FOR THE WIDTH OF THE LID.

WESTERN R's

THE SAN FRANCISCO GLASS HOUSES EMPLOYED A MOLD MAKER THAT MADE HIS R's IN A DISTICTIVE STYLE. THEY HAD A CURVED LEG. THESE APPEAR ON BOTTLES BLOWN FROM THE 1870 TO EARLY 1880 ERA. THET APPEAR ON ALMOST EVERY STYLE OF WESTERN BLOWN BOTTLE. SOME BOTTLES THAT HAVE THEM ALSO HAVE A SIMILAR BOTTLE WITHOUT THEM. THESE HAD A DIFFERENT MOLD OR WERE BLOWN AT A DIFFERENT GLASS HOUSE. THESE TYPES OF R's ALSO APPEAR ON PONTIL ERA EASTERN BLOWN BOTTLES BUT ARE NOT QUITE THE SAME. CLOSE INSPECTION WILL REVEAL THIS. THIS DETAIL HELPED TO IDENTIFY MANY BOTTLES WHOSE POINT OF OIRGIN WAS NOT KNOWN. SEE SOME EXAMPLES BELOW.

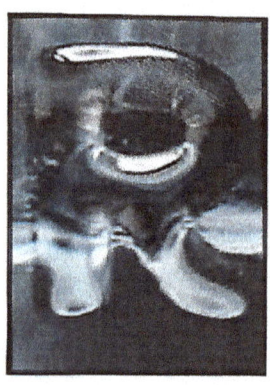 

EARLY STYLE CITRATE of MAGNESIA BOTTLES

ABRAMSON & BACON / CITRATE / OF / MAGNESIA / S.F.
(in round plate)

> TOOLED TOP, ROUNDED BASE
> CLEAR
> EX. RARE

FRANK B. ANGELL / DRUGGIST / NEAR UNION DEPOT / DENVER, COLO. *(in round plate)*

> TOOLED TOP, ROUNDED BASE
> AQUA
> RARE

C.W. ARMSTRONG / DRUGGIST / CALISTOGA, CAL.
(in round plate)

> TOOLED TOP, ROUNDED BASE
> CLEAR
> RARE

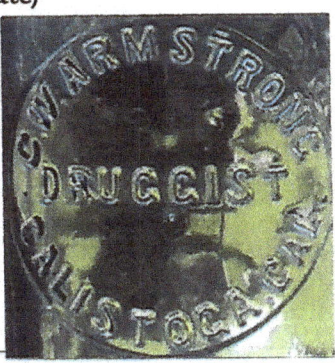

ARTHUR / LEADING DRUGGIST / GRAND JUNCTION, COLO. *(in round plate)*

> TOOLED TOP, ROUNDED BASE
> AQUA
> RARE

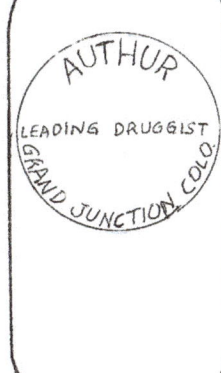

THE ASPEN PHARMACY / CITRATE / OF / MAGNESIA / ASPEN, COLORADO
(in round plate)

> TOOLED TOP, ROUNDED BASE
> CLEAR
> RARE

F.A. AUSTIN / CITRATE / OF / MAGNESIA / COLFAX & JOSEPHINE *(in round plate)*

> TOOLED TOP, ROUNDED BASE
> CLEAR
> RARE
> Locale: DENVER, COLO.

E.H. BAKER / DRUGS / 117 WEST / ST. CLARA ST. / SAN JOSE *(in fancy round plate)*

    TOOLED TOP, FLAT BASE
    AQUA
    RARE

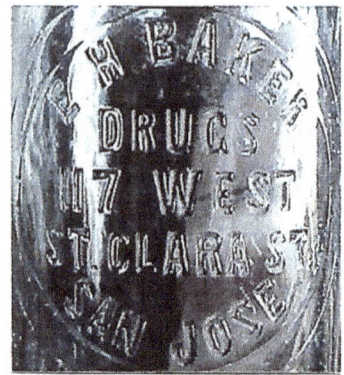

BEN L. BEAR / UP TO / DATE DRUGGIST / NAPA, CAL. *(in round plate)*

    TOOLED TOP, ROUNDED BASE
    COBALT, $950.00- 2020
    RARE

W.F. BENTE & CO. / CITRATE / OF / MAGNESIA / VICTOR, COLO. *(in round plate)*

    TOOLED TOP, ROUNDED BASE
    AQUA
    RARE

BEST'S / PHARMACY / CENTRAL CITY COLO. *(in fancy round plate)*

    EARLY TOOLED TOP, FLAT BASE
    CLEAR
    EX. RARE

CORNELIUS BEUKMA / PHARMACIST / DENVER

    TOOLED TOP, ROUNDED BASE
    AQUA
    RARE

THE BROADWAY PHARMACY / DENVER, COLORADO *(in round plate)*

    EARLY TOOLED TOP, FLAT BASE
    CLEAR
    RARE

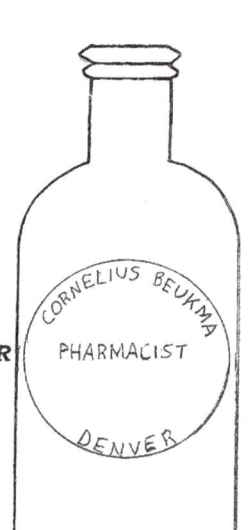
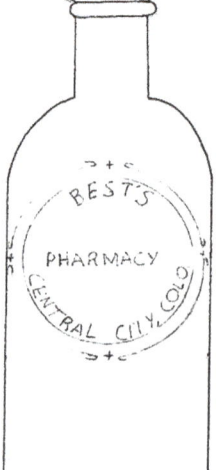

BOYSON'S PHARMACY / monogram / SAN FRANCISCO
(in round plate)

TOOLED TOP, ROUNDED BASE
COBALT, $300.00- 2020
Varient: B ONLY, FOR MONOGRAM
BOTH VARIENTS ARE EX. RARE

BOSTON DRUG STORE / mortar & pestle / SACRAMENTO (in fancy round plate)

TOOLED TOP, FLAT BASE
LT. AMETHYST
EX. RARE, $150.00- 2003
Note: THIS BOTTLE IS NOT A WHITALL TATUM
BLOWN BOTTLE LIKE MOST CITRATE
BOTTLES ARE. IT IS A LITTLE SMALLER
WITH A SOMEWHAT DIFFERENT TOP.

H. BOWMAN & CO. / PHARMACISTS / OAKLAND CAL.
(in fancy round plate)

EARLY TOOLED TOP, FLAT BASE
COBALT, $300.00- 2020
RARE

H. BOWMAN / DRUGGIST / OAKLAND
(in round plate)

EARLY TOOLED TOP, FLAT BASE
COBALT, $425.00- 2020
RARE
Note: AD CIRCA 1874
FROM THE OAKLAND
CITY DIRECTORY.
HENRY BOWMAN HAD
MOVED FROM
SACRAMENTO, A FEW
YEARS EARLIER.

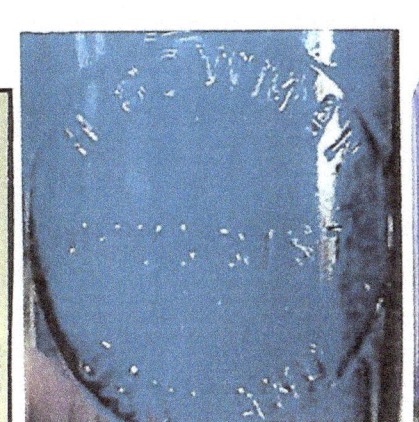

BOWMAN & SON / PHARMACISTS / OAKLAND
(in fancy round plate)

    EARLY TOOLED TOP, FLAT BASE
    COBALT
    RARE

**B. BROEMMEL / monogram, mortar & pestle /
N.W. COR. 6th & MISSION, S.F.**
(in fancy round plate)

    EARLY TOOLED TOP, FLAT BASE
    AQUA
    EX. RARE

**BUKER & COLSON / WILL PAY / 5 / CENTS / FOR
THIS BOTTLE** *(in round plate)*

    TOOLED TOP, ROUNDED BASE
    AQUA
    RARE
    Variant: COBALT, EX. RARE

**G.G. BURNETT / CITRATE / OF / MAGNESIA /
SAN FRANCISCO** *(in fancy round plate)*

    EARLY TOOLED TOP, FLAT BASE
    AQUA RARE

J. CALIGARIS / GRANULATED / CITRATE OF MAGNESIA

    RECT., TOOLED TOP, 6 ¼"
    COBALT
    EX. RARE
    Locale: SAN FRANCISCO

CITRATE / J. CALIGARIS / MAGNESIA
    (in fancy round plate)

    EARLY TOOLED TOP, FLAT BASE
    AQUA
    SCARCE

CARSON – RILEY DRUG CO. / CITRATE / OF / MAGNESIA / SAN JOSE
    (in fancy round plate)

    EARLY TOOLED TOP, FLAT BASE
    CLEAR
    RARE

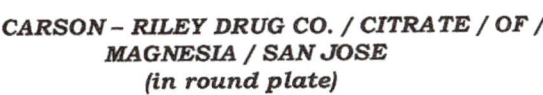

CARSON – RILEY DRUG CO. / CITRATE / OF / MAGNESIA / SAN JOSE
    (in round plate)

    TOOLED TOP, ROUNDED BASE
    COBALT, $400.00- 2020
    EX. RARE

A.W. CLARK / CITRATE / OF / MAGNESIA / DENVER, COLO. *(in round plate)*

    TOOLED TOP, ROUNDED BASE
    CLEAR
    RARE

J.C. CLAYWORTH / PHARMACIST / BENICIA, CAL. *(in round plate, with dosage above)*

    TOOLED TOP, ROUNDED BASE
    CLEAR
    EX. RARE

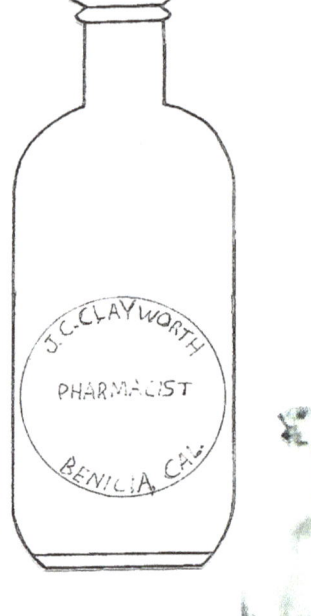 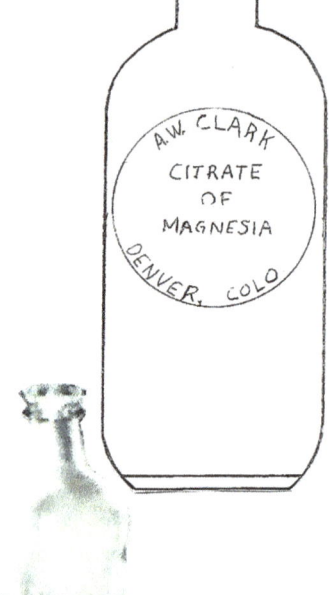

CITRATE / OF / MAGNESIA

    APPLIED TOP, FLAT BASE
    CLEAR FLINT GLASS
    SCARCE

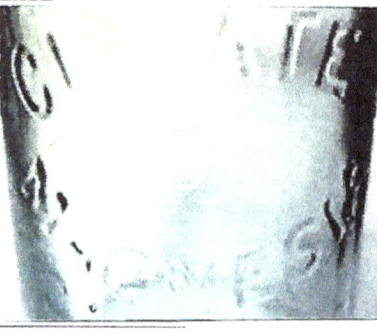

CITRATE / OF / MAGNESIA *(in fancy round plate)*

    APPLIED TOP, FLAT BASE
    SHADES of BLUE
    SCARCE

COFFIN & MAYHEW S.F. / CITRATE / OF / MAGNESIA *(in fancy round plate)*

    EARLY TOOLED TOP, FLAT BASE
    AQUA
    RARE

S.D. CUNNINGHAM / SILVERTON, COLO.
(in script)

    TOOLED TOP, ROUNDED BASE
    CLEAR
    EX. RARE

CITRATE / B.B. DAVID / CHEYENNE / OF MAGNESIA (in round plate)

    TOOLED TOP, FLAT BASE
    CLEAR
    EX. RARE

FRED C. EWING / CITY / DRUG STORE / COLO. / GLENWOOD SPRINGS
(in round plate)

    TOOLED TOP, ROUNDED BASE
    CLEAR
    RARE

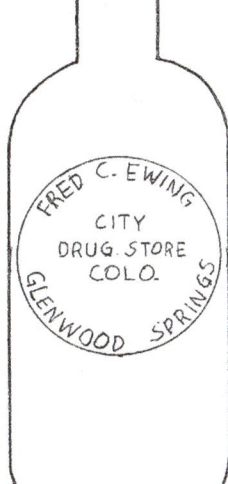

FAIRHAVEN / PHARMACY
(in fancy round plate)

    EARLY TOOLED TOP, FLAT BASE
    CLEAR
    EX. RARE
    Circa: 1890
    Locale: FAIRHAVEN, WASH.

S.W. CORNER / DAVID M. FLETCHER / VAN NESS AVE. & GEARY ST. (in round plate)

    TOOLED TOP, ROUNDED BASE
    AQUA
    RARE
    Locale: SAN FRANCISCO

FLINT & CRANE / CITRATE / MAGNESIA
(in fancy round plate)

    EARLY TOOLED TOP
    CLEAR
    EX. RARE
    Locale: MARYSVILLE, CAL.

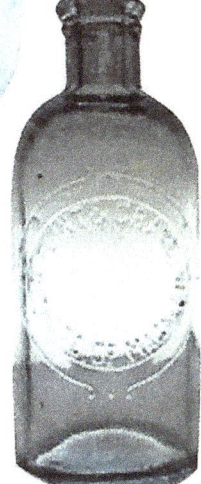

EDDY & CO. / CENTRAL / DRUG STORE / SONORA, CAL.
(in round plate, with dosage above)

    TOOLED TOP, ROUNDED BASE
    SCARCE
    AQUA, $70.00- 2013

FLINT & CRANE / CITRATE / MAGNESIA / MARYSVILLE, CAL.
(in fancy round plate)

    EARLY TOOLED TOP, FLAT BASE
    AQUA
    RARE

E.F. FORD / CITRATE / OF / MAGNESIA / PUEBLO, COLORADO *(in round plate)*

    TOOLED TOP, ROUNDED BASE
    AQUA
    RARE

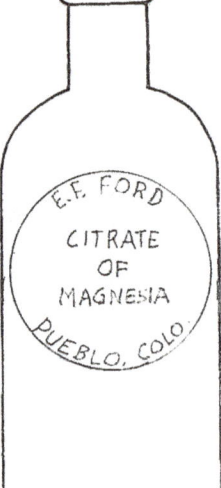

JAMES FROST / monogram / VALLEJO
(in round plate)

    APPLIED TOP, FLAT BASE
    AQUA, $230.00- 2020
    RARE
    Varient: EARLY TOOLED TOP

JUSTIN GATES / SACRAMENTO
(in fancy round plate)

    EARLY TOOLED TOP, FLAT BASE
    AQUA
    EX. RARE
    Locale: SACRAMENTO, CAL.

T.A. GREENLEAF / PALACE / DRUG STORE / SAN LUIS OBISPO *(in round plate)*

    TOOLED TOP, ROUND BASE
    EX. RARE
    COBALT, $2200.00- 2017, $1300.00- 2020

THE UNIVERSITY STORE / ALFRED A. GREENMAN / BOULDER, COLO. *(in round plate)*

    TOOLED TOP, ROUNDED BASE
    CLEAR,
    RARE

G.F. HATCH / CITRATE / OF / MAGNESIA / DENVER, COLO. *(in round plate)*

    TOOLED TOP, ROUNDED BASE
    CLEAR
    RARE

HEUSSY & FILZ / SEATTLE / WASH. *(in round plate)*

    TOOLED TOP, ROUNDED BASE
    AQUA
    EX. RARE

F.M. HILBY / PHARMACIST / MONTEREY, CAL. *(in round plate)*

    TOOLED TOP, ROUNDED BASE
    CLEAR
    RARE

**F.J. HILL & CO. / CITRATE / OF / MAGNESIA /
SALT LAKE CITY** *(in fancy round plate)*

   TOOLED TOP, FLAT BASE
   CLEAR
   EX. RARE

**C.E. HINCKLEY & CO. / APOTHECARIES /
SAN FRANCISCO**

   APPLIED TOP, FLAT BASE
   RARE
   DEEP AQUA
   GREEN, $1100.00- 2020
   Note: AD BELOW is from 1863

**DR. J.J. HOGAN / NEXT TO THE POST
OFFICE / VALLEJO, CAL.**
(in round plate)

   TOOLED TOP, ROUNDED BASE
   COBALT
   EX. RARE

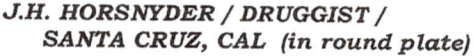

**J.H. HORSNYDER / DRUGGIST /
SANTA CRUZ, CAL** *(in round plate)*

   TOOLED TOP, ROUNDED BASE
   CLEAR
   RARE

**THE HORNUNG DRUG STORE / ESTABLISHED
1855 / MARYSVILLE, CAL.**
(in round plate)

   TOOLED TOP, ROUNDED BASE
   CLEAR
   EX. RARE

HEUSSY DRUG CO. / SEATTLE / WASH.
(in round plate)

  TOOLED TOP, ROUNDED BASE
  CLEAR
  RARE

D.D. HUNT / 1800 / HAIGHT ST. / SAN FRANCISCO *(in round plate)*

  TOOLED TOP, ROUNDED BASE
  AQUA
  RARE

WM. H. KEITH & CO. / APOTHECARIES / SAN FRANCISCO

  APPLIED TOP, FLAT BASE
  AQUA, 7" and 6 ¼", $1200.00- 2020
  (lot of 2)
  COMES IN AT LEAST 4 SIZES FROM 5" to 7 ½"
  SCARCE IN ALL SIZES WITH THE SMALLEST
    BEING THE RAREST.
  THE LARGE SIZE HAS A MOLD LINE AROUND
    THE BODY ABOUT ½" FROM THE BASE.
  Note: THE AD BELOW RIGHT is from the 1865
    S.F. DIRECTORY.

KELLER – BOHMANSSON / DRUG CO.
(in round plate with dosage above)

  TOOLED TOP, ROUNDED BASE
  CLEAR
  SCARCE
  Locale: EUREKA, CAL.

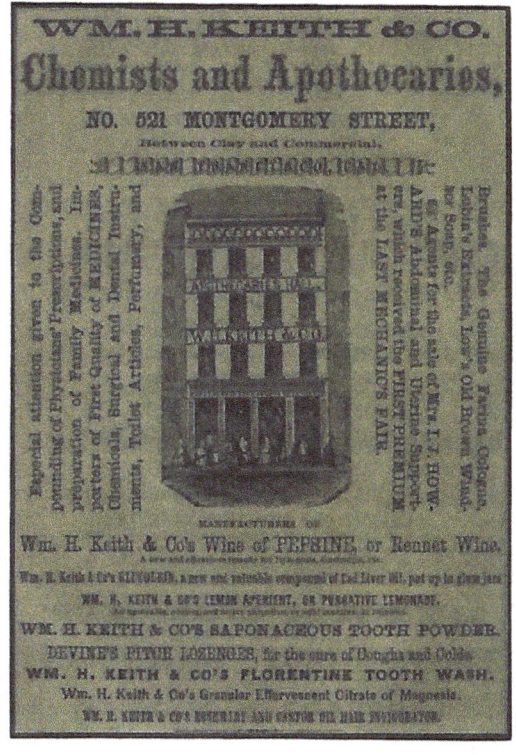

KROUGH'S / SALINAS, CAL. *(in round plate)*

>   *TOOLED TOP, ROUNDED BASE*
>   *AQUA*
>   *RARE*

A.L. LENGFELD / BALDWIN / PHARMACY / MARKET, POWELL & EDDY STS. S.F.
(in fancy round plate)

>   *EARLY TOOLED TOP, FLAT BASE*
>   *AQUA*
>   *RARE*

A.L. LENGFELD / PHARMACIST / COR. GEARY & STOCKTON STS. S.F.
(in fancy round plate)

>   *EARLY TOOLED TOP, FLAT BASE*
>   *AQUA*
>   *EX. RARE*

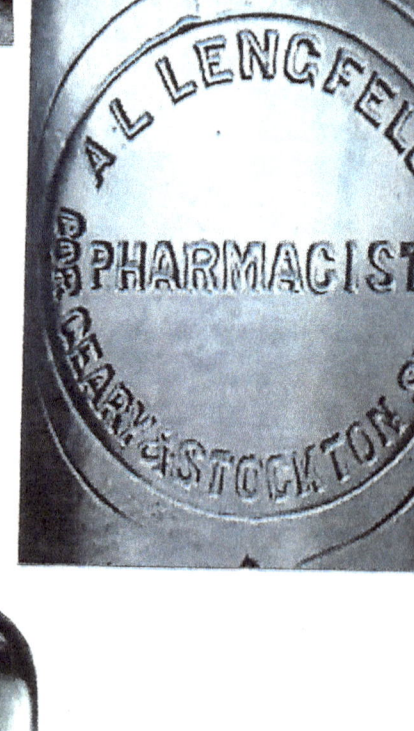

LENGFELD'S / PRESCRIPTION / PHARMACY / SAN FRANCISCO
(in fancy round plate)

>   *EARLY TOOLED TOP, FLAT BASE*
>   *AQUA*
>   *RARE*

AL.S. LAMB / lamb / ASPEN, COLO.
(in round plate)

>   *TOOLED TOP, ROUNDED BASE*
>   *AQUA*
>   *EX. RARE*

**LENGFELD'S / PRESCRIPTION / PHARMACIES /
SAN FRANCISCO** *(in round plate)*

    TOOLED TOP, RUNDED BASE
    AQUA
    COBALT, $400.00- 2020
    BOTH are EX. RARE

G.R. LEWIS & CO. *(in round plate)*

    TOOLED TOP, ROUNDED BASE
    CLEAR
    RARE
    Locale: CRIPPLE CREEK, COLO.

**F.J. LORD / CITRATE / OF / MAGNESIA /
DENVER, COLO.** *(in round plate)*

    TOOLED TOP, ROUNDED BASE
    AQUA
    RARE

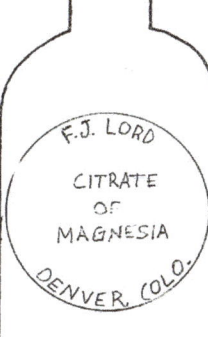  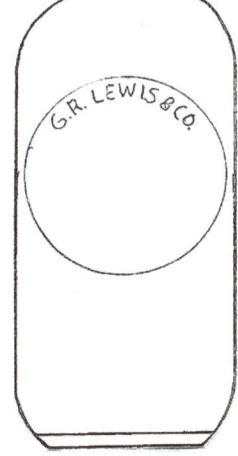

**McKENZIE BROS. / PHARMACISTS /
LEADVILLE, COLO.** *(in round plate)*

    TOOLED TOP, ROUNDED BASE
    AQUA
    RARE

JAS. McDONNELL / S.F. / CITRATE OF MAGNESIA
              (in fancy round plate)

    EARLY TOOLED TOP, FLAT BASE
    AQUA
    EX. RARE

WM. MOORE / (monogram) / STOCKTON, CAL.
(in round plate)

    TOOLED TOP, ROUNDED BASE
    CLEAR
    EX. RARE

G.A. MOREHEAD / CITRATE / OF / MAGNESIA /
WATSONVILLE, CAL. (in round plate)

    TOOLED TOP, ROUNDED BASE
    EX. RARE
    COBALT, $1200.00- 2018, $425.00- 2020

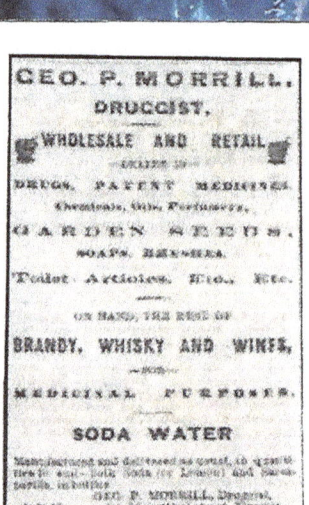

GEO. P. MORRILL / APOTHECARY /
VIRGINIA CITY

    APPLIED TOP, FLAT BASE
    EX. RARE
    DEEP AQUA, $2600.00- 2007

MITCHELL'S / EFFERVESENT / MAGNESIA

    RECT, TOOLED TOP, 5 ¼"
    AMBER
    EX. RARE
    Note: THIS BOTTLE WAS DUG IN NEVADA
          AND MAY BE ENGLISH IN ORIGIN.
          IT CLOSELY RESEMBLES THE
          J. CALIGARIS RECT. BOTTLE FROM S.F.

PACIFIC PHARMACY / EUREKA, CAL.
(in round plate)

    TOOLED TOP, ROUNDED BASE
    CLEAR
    SCARCE

NICOLAI'S / PHARMACY / LEADVILLE / COLO. *(in round plate)*

    TOOLED TOP, ROUNDED BASE
    AQUA
    RARE

S.A. PALMER / DRUGGIST / SANTA CRUZ, CAL.
(in round plate)

    TOOLED TOP, ROUNDED BASE
    AMBER, $350.00- 2020
    EX. RARE

PATTERSON'S / PHARMACY / E. MAIN ST. 44 / STOCKTON, CAL. *(in round plate)*

    TOOLED TOP, ROUNDED BASE
    CLEAR
    EX. RARE

W.S. PARKINSON / DRUGGIST / GLENWOOD SPRINGS *(in round plate)*

    TOOLED TOP, ROUNDED BASE
    CLEAR
    RARE

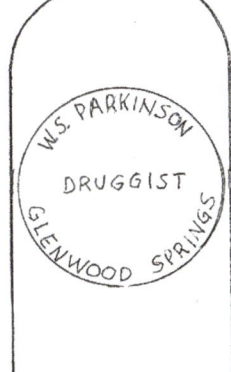

PEARSE & McGILL / CITRATE / OF / MAGNESIA / CHEYENNE, WYO. *(in fancy round plate)*

    EARLY TOOLED TOP, FLAT BASE
    CLEAR
    EX. RARE

W. PFUNDER / baby's head / PORTLAND
(in fancy round plate)

    EARLY TOOLED TOP, FLAT BASE
    AQUA
    EX. RARE

HIRAM POND / PHARMACIST / HOLLISTER, CAL. (in round plate)

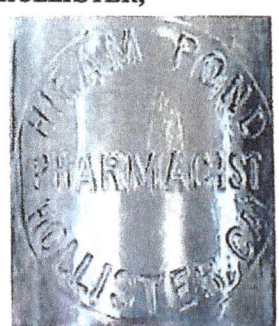

    TOOLED TOP, ROUNDED BASE
    AQUA
    RARE

THE QUAKER DRUG CO. / (INCORPORATED) / 1013 – 1015 / FIRST AVE. / SEATTLE, WASH. (in round plate)

    TOOLED TOP, ROUNDED BASE
    COBALT
    EX. RARE
    CIRCA: 1901
    Note: THIS IS THE ONLY COBALT WASHINGTON CITRATE BOTTLE.

RAWLINS / CONSOLIDATED DRUG CO. / CITRATE / OF / MAGNESIA / RAWLINS, WYO.
(in fancy round plate)

    TOOLED TOP, ROUNDED BASE
    AQUA
    RARE

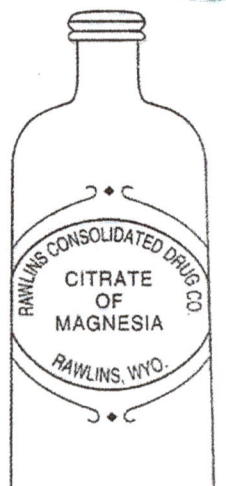

RED CROSS PHARMACY / EUREKA, CAL.
(in round plate)

    TOOLED TOP, ROUNDED BASE
    CLEAR
    SCARCE

RHODES & TROXELL / CHEYENNE, WYO. / PRESCRIPTION DRUGGISTS
(in fancy round plate)

    TOOLED TOP, FLAT BASE
    CLEAR
    EX. RARE

RUBEL & BOULTON / PHARMACISTS / MARYSVILLE, CAL. *(in round plate)*

    TOOLED TOP, ROUNDED BASE
    CLEAR
    EX. RARE

W.R. SAMSON / DRUGGIST / DENVER COLO. *(in round plate)*

    TOOLED TOP, ROUNDED BASE
    CLEAR
    RARE

J.B. SCOTT / PHARMACIST / SALINAS *(in round plate)*

    TOOLED TOP, ROUNDED BASE
    CLEAR
    RARE

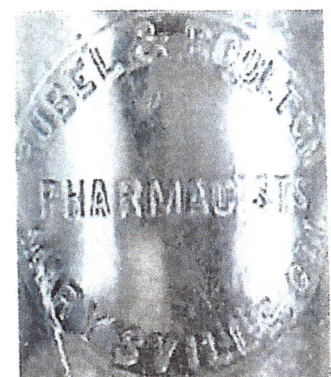

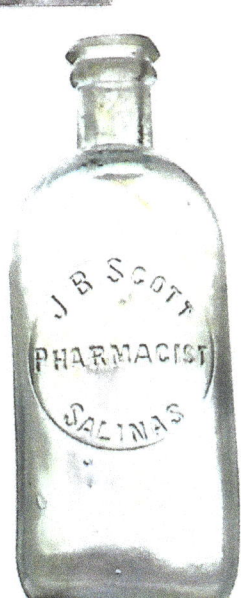

A. SCHOPPE / CITRATE / OF / MAGNESIA / DENVER, COLO. *(in round plate)*

    TOOLED TOP, ROUNDED BASE
    CLEAR
    RARE

FRED C. SHAW / OPPOSITE / BROWN PALACE / HOTEL / DENVER *(in round plate)*

    TOOLED TOP, ROUNDED BASE
    AQUA
    RARE

B.F. SHAW / VIRGINIA CITY, NEV. *(in round plate)*

    TOOLED TOP, ROUNDED BASE
    EX. RARE
    AQUA, $550.00- 2009
    Note: HAS DOSAGE ABOVE PLATE

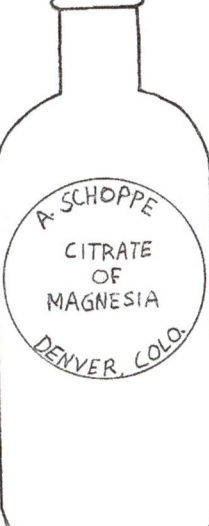

S.G. SKIDMORE / 111 FIRST ST. / PORTLAND
(in round plate)

    EARLY TOOLED TOP, FLAT BASE
    AQUA
    EX. RARE

R.W. SKINNER & CO. / PHARMACISTS / EUREKA, CAL. (in round plate)

    TOOLED TOP, ROUNDED BASE
    CLEAR
    SCARCE

C.H. SKINNER / CITRATE / OF / MAGNESIA / COR. 1st & BROADWAY (in round plate)

    TOOLED TOP, ROUNDED BASE
    AQUA
    RARE
    Locale: DENVER, COLO.

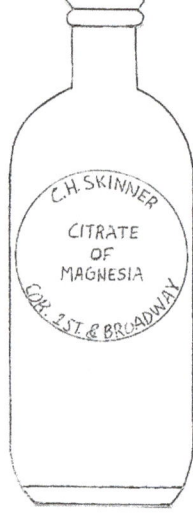

A.H. SMITH & CO. / monogram / POLK & BUSH STS. (in fancy round plate)

    EARLY TOOLED TOP, FLAT BASE
    CLEAR
    EX. RARE
    Locale: SAN FRANCICSO

SMITH & DAVIS / DRUGGISTS / PORTLAND / OREGON

    APPLIED TOP, FLAT BASE
    EX. RARE
    AQUA, $100.00- 2006
    Note: AD at RIGHT is from
    THE 1867 S.F. DIRECTORY

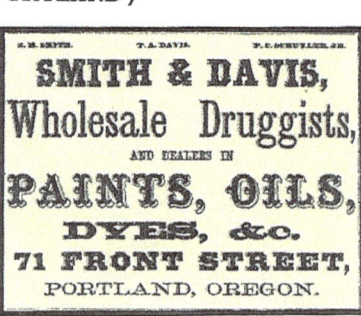

W.H. SMITH / PHARMACIST / ST. HELENA, CAL. (in round plate)

    TOOLED TOP, ROUNDED BASE
    COBALT, $170.00- 2020 (damaged)
    EX. RARE

J.G. STEELE & CO. / SAN FRANCISCO

APPLIED TOP, FLAT BASE
DEEP AQUA, $650.00- 2020
GREEN
RARE in BOTH COLORS
Note: THIS is the WESTERN
 BLOWN VARIENT.
Note: AD at RIGHT is FROM
 1871 S.F. DIRECTORY.

J.G. STEELE & CO. / SAN FRANCISCO

EARLY TOOLED TOP, FLAT BASE
LT. AQUA
RARE
Note: THIS is the EASTERN
 BLOWN VARIENT.

C.E. SMITH / DRUGGIST / COLORADO
 SPRINGS, COLO. *(in fancy round plate)*

EARLY TOOLED TOP, FLAT BASE
CLEAR
EX. RARE

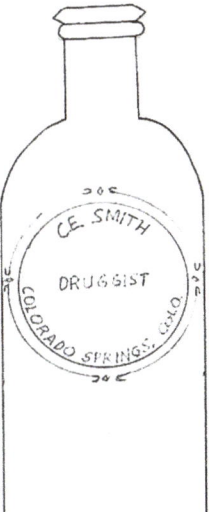

STEWART & HOLMES / DRUG CO. / TACOMA
 (in fancy round plate)

EARLY TOOLED TOP, FLAT BASE
AQUA
RARE

STEWART & HOLMES / DRUG CO. / SEATTLE,
 WASH. *(in round plate)*

TOOLED TOP, ROUNDED BASE
CLEAR
RARE

**STEWART & HOLMES / DRUG CO. / WALLA
WALLA, WASH.** *(in fancy round plate)*

EARLY TOOLED TOP, FLAT BASE
CLEAR
EX. RARE

STOCKTON DRUG CO. / STOCKTON, CAL.
(in round plate)

TOOLED CROWN TOP, ROUNDED BASE
SCARCE
DEEP GREEN, $70.00- 2009
Note: ALTHOUGH THIS BOTTLE IS NOT
 AS OLD AS THE OTHERS IN THIS
 SECTION, I WANTED TO INCLUDE
 IT BECAUSE OF THE RARE COLOR.

**F.M. STREAMER / DRUGGIST / BOULDER,
COLO.** *(in fancy round plate)*

EARLY TOOLED TOP, FLAT BASE
AMBER
EX. RARE

**STREAMER & WHITNEY / CITRATE
MAGNESIA / BOULDER**
(in fancy round plate)

EARLY TOOLED TOP, FLAT BASE
COBALT
EX. RARE
Locale: BOULDER, COLO.

L.L. TALLMAN / DRUGGIST / WALLA WALLA
(in round plate)

TOOLED TOP, ROUNDED BASE
CLEAR
RARE

JAMES TOPLEY / GEORGIA ST. / VALLEJO
(in fancy round plate)

EARLY TOOLED TOP, FLAT BASE
COMMON in AQUA
EX. RARE in COBALT
Varient: HAS THE NEWER STYLE
 TOOLED TOP

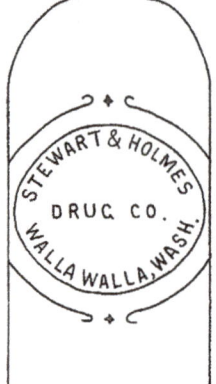

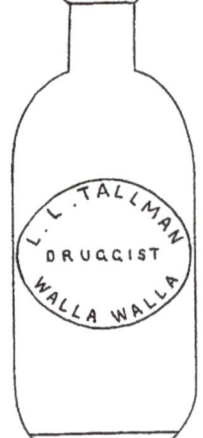
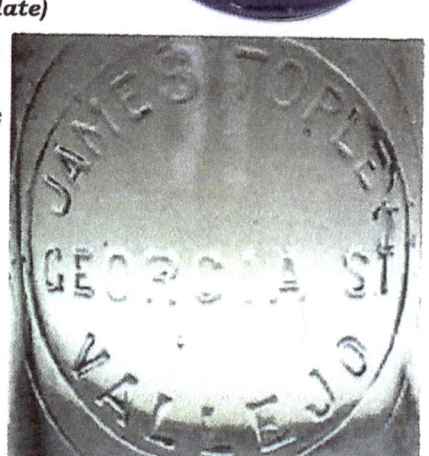

OTTO TRAUTZ / monogram / BENICIA, CAL.
(in fancy round plate)

    TOOLED TOP, FLAT BASE
    EX. RARE
    COBALT, $1500.00- 2017
               $750.00- 2020

TRUNK BROS. / TEL 894 / DRUGGISTS / trunk / OPEN ALL NIGHT / COR. 16th & TREMONT STS. / DENVER, COLO. *(in round plate)*

    TOOLED TOP, ROUNDED BASE
    CLEAR
    RARE

ED. F. TRUNK / DRUGGIST / trunk / OPEN ALL NIGHT / COR. 16th & / TREMONT STS. / DENVER
(in round plate)

    TOOLED TOP, ROUNDED BASE
    CLEAR
    RARE

CHAS. K. TUTTLE / DRUGGIST / PACIFIC GROVE, CAL.
(in round plate)

    TOOLED TOP, ROUNDED BASE
    AQUA
    EX. RARE

THE UNIVERSITY BOOK & DRUG STORE / C / BOULDER, COLO.
(in round plate)

    TOOLED TOP, ROUNDED BASE
    CLEAR
    RARE

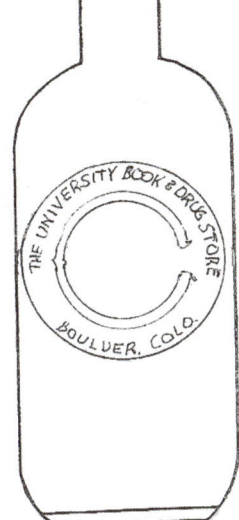

CITRATE OF MAGNESIA / H.P. WAKELEE & CO. / DRUGGIST
(embossed vertically)

    APPLIED TOP, FLAT BASE
    RARE
    COBALT, $600.00- 2007, $400.00- 2020

CITRATE OF MAGNESIA / H.P. WAKELEE / DRUGGIST
(embossed vertically)

    APPLIED BLOB TOP, FLAT BASE
    SCARCE
    COBALT, $950.00- 2020

WAKELEE & CO. / monogram / SAN FRANCISCO
(in fancy round plate)

    EARLY TOOLED TOP
    FLAT BASE
    COBALT, $160.00- 2020
    EX. RARE

WAKELEE & CO. / monogram / SAN FRANCISCO
(in round plate)

    TOOLED TOP, ROUNDED BASE
    COBALT, $275.00- 2020
    EX. RARE

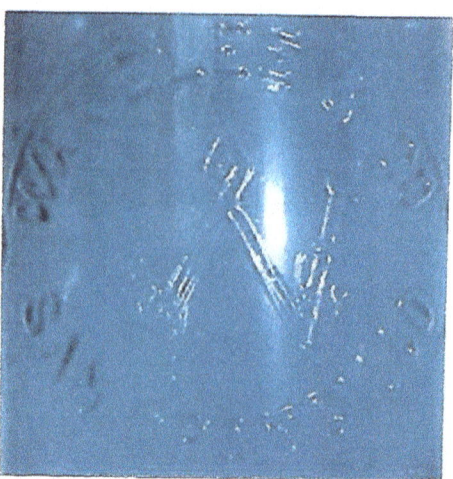
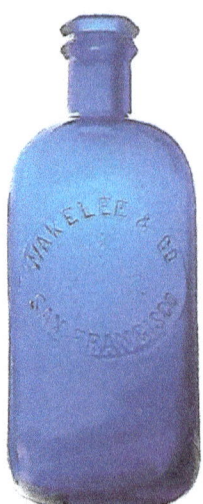

H.P. WAKELEE / SAN FRANCISCO
   (embossed vertically)

   APPLIED TOP, FLAT BASE
   7" and 7 ½" TALL
   AQUA, $100.00- 2020 (lot of 2)
   SCARCE

WAKELEE & CO. / monogram / SAN FRANCISCO
   (in fancy round plate)

   EARLY TOOLED TOP, FLAT BASE
   COBALT
   EX. RARE

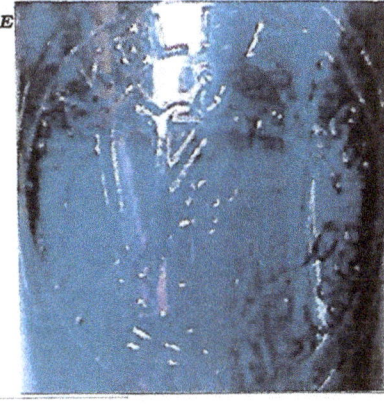

WAKELEE'S / PHARMACIES / SAN FRANCISCO
   (in round plate)

   TOOLED TOP, ROUNDED BASE
   AQUA
   DEEP GREEN, $1100.00- 2020
   BOTH COLORS are RARE

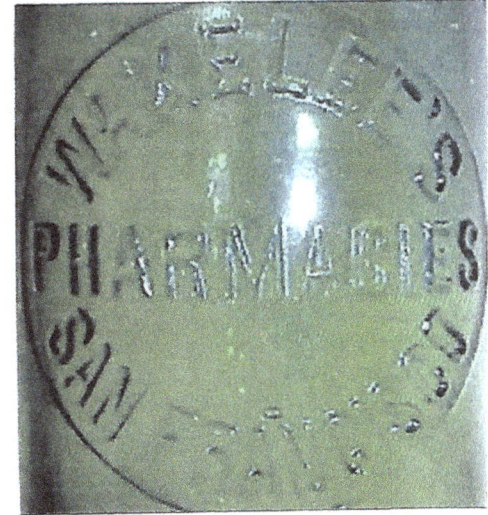
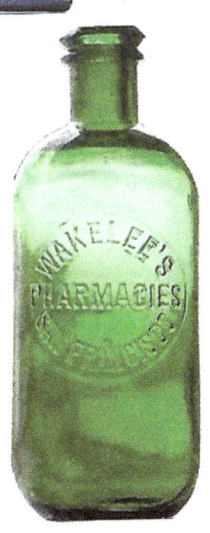

R.E. WHITE & CO. / APOTHECARIES S.F.
   (in fancy round plate)

   TOOLED TOP, ROUNDED BASE
   RARE
   CLEAR, $120.00- 2006

C.H. WELLS & CO. / DRUGGISTS / PUEBLO, COLORADO
(in round plate)

    TOOLED TOP, ROUNDED BASE
    AQUA
    RARE

THE WHITNEY – BLAKE / CITRATE / OF / MAGNESIA / PHARMACY
(in round plate)

    TOOLED TOP, RUNDED BASE
    AQUA
    RARE
    Locale: BOULDER, COLO.

WINDSOR PHARMACY / OPEN ALL NIGHT / GRAVES & SCOTT
(in fancy round plate)

    EARLY TOOLED TOP, FLAT BASE
    CLEAR
    EX. RARE
    Locale: DENVER, COLO.

WISDOM'S / SOL. CITRATE / MAGNESIA
(in fancy round plate)

    EARLY TOOLED TOP, FLAT BASE
    AQUA
    RARE
    Locale: PORTLAND, OREGON

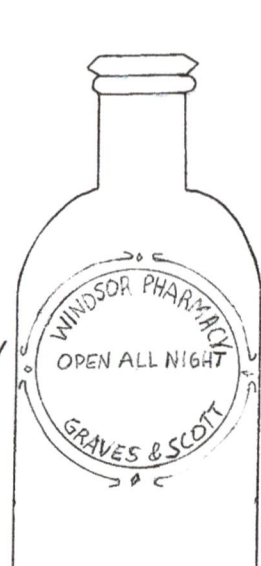
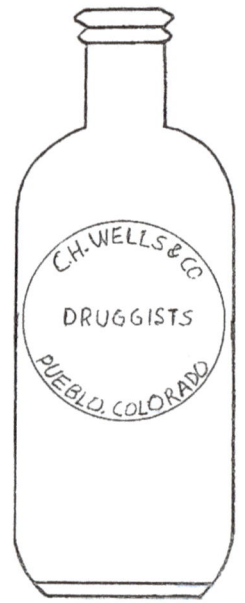
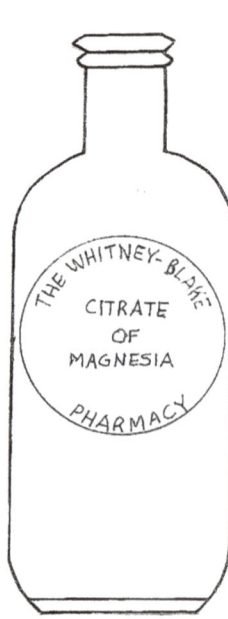

WOODWARD, CLARK & CO. / DRUGGISTS / PORTLAND, OR. *(in round plate)*

    TOOLED TOP, ROUNDED BASE
    CLEAR
    RARE

WYNKOOP – VAUGH CO. / DRUGGISTS / TACOMA, WASH. *(in round plate)*

    TOOLED TOP, ROUND BASE
    CLEAR
    RARE

C.L. WILHELM / SAN FRANCISCO
(in round plate)

EARLY TOOLED TOP, FLAT BASE
AQUA
SCARCE

LATE ADDITIONS to the CITRATE SECTION

BENSON, SMITH & CO. / HONOLULU, HI.
(in round plate)

TOOLED TOP, ROUNDED BASE
AQUA
RARE

STRAHLMANN & CO. / DRUGGISTS / SAN DIEGO, CAL.
(in round plate)

TOOLED TOP, ROUNDED BASE
AQUA
EX. RARE, $400.00- 2002

EDWARD A. BAER / SOUTHERN PHARMACY / BAKERSFIELD, CAL. *(in round plate)*

TOOLED TOP, ROUNDED BASE
COBALT, $300.00- 2020 (bruise)
EX. RARE

COSMETIC, SKIN LOTION TYPE BOTTLES

Front: AINAXAB / CELEBRATED EGYPIAN / ELIXIR FOR THE SKIN / A.J. GIRARDIN & CO. / SAN FRANCISCO

    SQUARE, SMOOTH BASE, 5 ½" and 6 ¼"
    TOOLED TOP
    CLEAR
    RARE
    Note: FIRST ADVERTISED IN 1881. AD AT RIGHT FROM THE 1894 S.F. DIRECTORY. THE AD BOTTOM RIGHT IS FROM THE NAPA VALLEY REGISTER AND SHOWS REDINGTON & CO. AS THE AGENTS IN 1885.

Front: ARABALINE LOTION / MFD. BY / THE ARABALINE CO. / S.F.

    RECT., SMOOTH BASE, 4 ½"
    TOOLED TOP
    CLEAR
    SCARCE

Front: BOWMAN'S / BEAUTIFUL SNOW / FOR THE COMPLEXION

    RECT., SMOOTH BASE, 5"
    TOOLED TOP
    COBALT
    RARE
    Locale: OAKLAND, CAL.
    Note: LABEL TRADE MARKED IN 1883 BY H. BOWMAN, OAKLAND, CAL. SEE BELOW. AD IS FROM THE 1875 OAKLAND DIRECTORY.

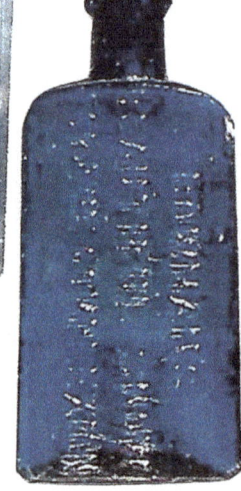

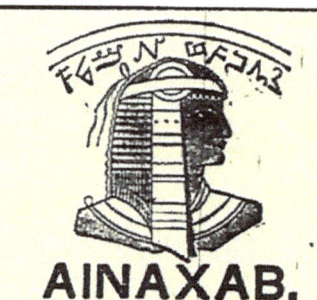

Front: **ALFALFA CREAM / JOY'S PHARMACY / LA JUNTA COLO.**

    RECT., SMOOTH BASE, 5 ½"
    TOOLED TOP
    CLEAR
    RARE

Front: **BARNES' / ALMOND CREAM**

    RECT., SMOOTH BASE, 5"
    TOOLED TOP, CLEAR
    SCARCE
    Locale: DENVER, COLO.

Front: **CHARLES D. BARNES / SNOW CREAM**

    RECT., SMOOTH BASE, 5"
    TOOLED TOP, CLEAR
    SCARCE
    Locale: DENVER, COLO.

Side: **CRÈME DE CAMELIA / FOR THE COMPLEXION**
Side: **THE BORADENT CO. INC / SAN FRANCISCO, NEW YORK**

    RECT., SMOOTH BASE, 5" and 2 ½"
    TOOLED TOP
    COBALT
    COMMON in the 5" SIzE
    SAMPLE SIZE is SCARCE
    Varient: NEW YORK is SLUGGED OUT

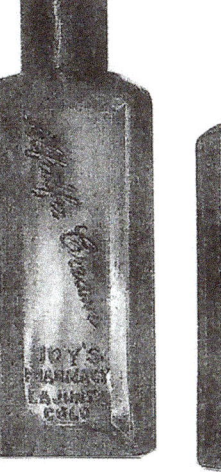

Front: **CHEATHAM'S / PEARL ROSE CREAM / MADE IN RENO**

    RECT., SMOOTH BASE, 4 ½"
    TOOLED TOP
    CLEAR
    RARE

Front: **CIRCASSIAN BLOOM**

    OVAL, SMOOTH BASE, 5"
    TOOLED TOP, CLEAR
    SCARCE
    CIRCA: 1892
    Note: J.J. MACK WAS THE AGENT FOR THIS BRAND IN S.F. SEE TRADE CARD BELOW.

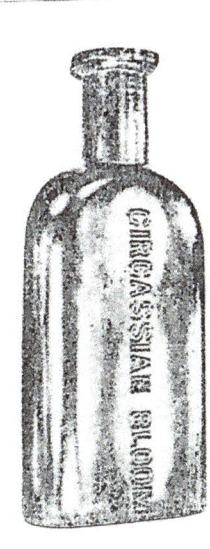

DICKEY / PIONEER / 1850 / mortar & pestle / CHEMIST / S.F.

RECT., SMOOTH BASE, 5 ½" to 6 ½"
APPLIED and TOOLED TOPS
AMBER, AQUA, TEAL, CLEAR and BLUE
RARITY VARIES GREATLY IN THE MANY
  COLORS and TOP FINISHES
DARK BLUE WITH A TOOLED TOP ARE RARE
SHADES of BLUE WITH APPLIED TOPS
  ARE COMMON
AMBER WITH A TOOLED TOP ARE COMMON
AMBER WITH APPLIED TOP ARE RARE
CLEAR, AQUA and TEAL ARE EX. RARE.
EARLIER VARIENTS HAVE A FLAT BASE OR
  A SQUARE INDENT.
SAPPHIRE BLUE, A.T., $90.00- 2019
DEEP COBALT, T.T., $250.00- 2019
MED. COBALT, T.T., FLAT BASE,
          $1000.00- 2017
LT. GREEN / AQUA, T.T., FLAT BASE,
          $3000.00- 2017
Note: ADS from 1864 and 1867 at RIGHT

 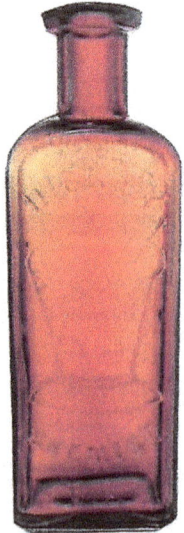   

Front: **COLORADO CREAM / MANUFACTERED BY / THE D.Y. BUTCHER DRUG CO.**

    RECT., SMOOTH BASE, 4 ½"
    TOOLED TOP, CLEAR
    SCARCE

Front: **BENZOATED / WITCH HAZEL CREAM / CREWS – BEGGS CO. PUEBLO**

    RECT., SMOOTH BASE, 4 ¾"
    TOOLED TOP, CLEAR
    SCARCE

Front: **GALLINGER'S / PEARL / CREAM / GALLINGER / & / AULT / GOLDFIELD / COLO.**

    RECT., SMOOTH BASE, 5"
    TOOLED TOP, CLEAR
    RARE

Front: **GUTMANN'S / DRY CLIMATE CREAM / F.L. GUTMANN / COLORADO SPRINGS, COLO.**

    RECT., SMOOTH BASE, 5"
    TOOLED TOP, CLEAR
    SCARCE

Front: **DAMASCUS / TRADE MARK / STODDART BROS. / COR. GEARY & MASON STS. / SAN FRANCISCO**
    (city, knight, camel in center)

    RECT., SMOOTH BASE, 4 ½"
    TOOLED TOP
    AMBER
    RARE
    Note: THIS BRAND WAS FIRST TRADE MARKED IN 1883 BY THE STODDART BROS. IN SAN FRANCISCO.

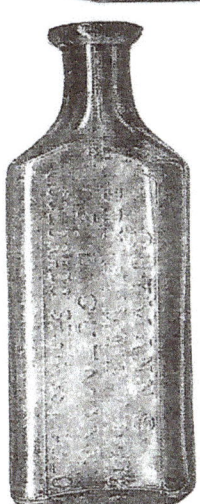

Front: FACIO CRÈME / THE GREAT SKIN BEAUTIFIER /
M'F'D BY / GILLEN & TREZONA /
SANTA CRUZ, CAL.

    RECT., SMOOTH BASE, 4 ¾:
    TOOLED TOP
    TEAL GREEN, $220.00- 2020
    EX. RARE

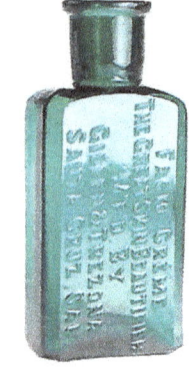

Front: motif of hand / GUTMAN'S / DRY CLIMATE
CREAM / D.E. MONROE & CO. /
COLORADO SPRINGS, COLO.

    RECT., SMOOTH BASE, 5"
    TOOLED TOP
    CLEAR
    SCARCE

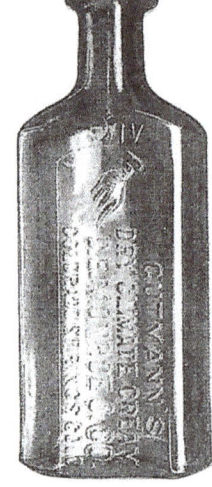

Front: MAYHEW & WENZELL / SAN FRANCISCO

    RECT., SMOOTH BASE, 6"
    EARLY TOOLED TOP
    EX. RARE, POSSIBLY UNIQUE
    COBALT, $950.00- 2004
    CIRCA: 1860's
    Note: THIS BOTTLE PROBABLY CONTAINED A
        COSMETIC, CONSIDERING WILLIAM
        WENZELL'S BUSINESS RELATIONSHIP
        WITH GEORGE DICKEY, WHO PRODUCED
        THE FAMOUS DICKEY PIONEER 1850
        BOTTLE THAT HAD A COMPLEXION
        PRODUCT IN IT.

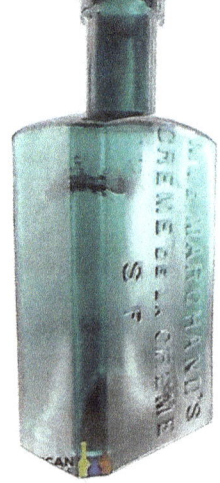

Front: MME. MARCHAND'S / CRÈME DE LA
CRÈME / S.F.

    RECT., SMOOTH BASE, 5"
    TOOLED TOP
    RARE
    DEEP TEAL GREEN, $240.00- 2017

Side: MmcDELISDINERE

    RECT., SMOOTH BASE, 5 ½"
    APPLIED and TOOLED TOP
    RARE
    COBALT, $325.00- 2019
    Note: HAS THE WESTERN CURVED R's

Front: McFARLAND'S / WHITE ROSE CRÈME /
SALIDA, COLORADO

    RECT., SMOOTH BASE, 4 ¾"
    TOOLED TOP
    CLEAR
    RARE

Front: **PAXON'S DERMALA**

    RECT., SMOOTH BASE, 6 ½"
    TOOLED TOP
    CLEAR
    SCARCE
    Locale: BUTTE, MONT.

Front: **PIONEER / 1850 / mortar & pestle**

    RECT., SMOOTH BASE, 6 – 6 ½"
    APPLIED, TOOLED and FLARED TOP
    AQUA, CLEAR
    EX. RARE
    COBALT, FLARED TOP, $2800.00- 2017
    Note: THIS IS THE EARLY VARIENT of the
    DICKEY PIONEER CHEMIST LINE

Front: **L.P. ROBINSON / DERMAL CREAM / SALT LAKE CITY**

    RECT., SMOOTH BASE, 4 ½"
    TOOLED TOP
    CLEAR
    SCARCE

Front: **SHAW'S / GLYCERINE / LOTION**

    RECT., SMOOTH BASE, 5"
    TOOLED TOP
    AQUA
    SCARCE
    Locale: SAN FRANCISCO

Front: **A.H. SMITH & CO. / AMARYLIS / FOR THE COMPLEXION / SAN FRANCISCO**

    RECT., SMOOTH BASE, 5 ½"
    TOOLED TOP
    COBALT
    RARE

Front: **U – AR – DAS / FOR THE COMPLEXION / PORTLAND, ORE.**

    RECT., SMOOTH BASE, 5"
    TOOLED TOP
    COBALT
    SCARCE

Front: **U – AR – DAS / FOR THE / COMPLEXION**
Side: **WOODWARD, CLARKE & CO.**
Side: **PORTLAND, OREGON**

    RECT., SMOOTH BASE, 5" and 2 ½"
    TOOLED TOP
    SCARCE
    COBALT, 5", $50.00- 2009
    COBALT, 2 ½", $50.00- 2009

Front: Motif of sun and shield / VALLEY TAN
REMEDIES
Side: C.E. JOHNSON
Side: SALT LAKE CITY

    OVAL, SMOOTH BASE, 6"
    TOOLED TOP
    AQUA
    SCARCE

Front: C.E. JOHNSON / MFG. / sun and shield /
VTR / SALT LAKE CITY / UTAH

    OVAL, SMOOTH BASE, 6"
    TOOLED TOP
    AQUA
    SCARCE

Front: WILLIAMS / BALSAMIC / CREAM OF ROSES
Base: S.F. & P.G.W.

    RECT., SMOOTH BASE, 5"
    TOOLED TOP
    COBALT
    RARE
    CIRCA: 1881
Note: THIS BRAND WAS FIRST TRADE MARKED in
1881 by JOHN R. WILLIAMS of STOCKTON.
SEE LABEL AT RIGHT. TRADE CARD at the
BOTTOM of PAGE, is PROBABLY THE SAME
TIME FRAME.

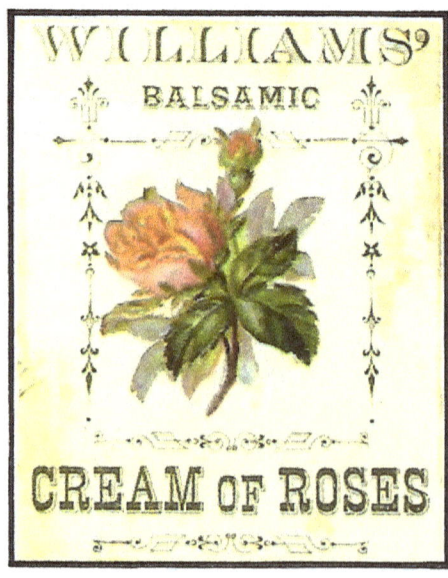

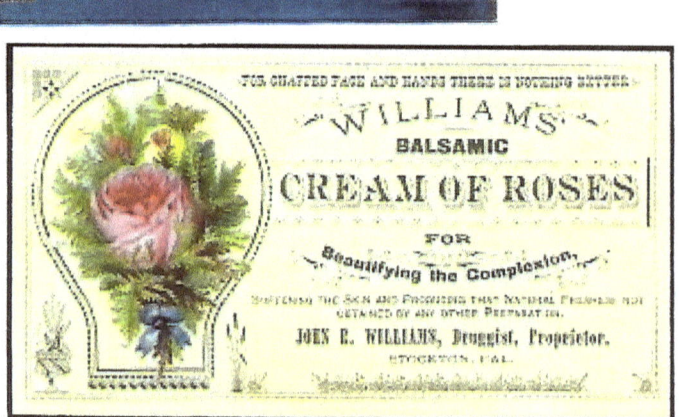

Front: WAKELEE'S / CAMELLINE

RECT., SMOOTH BASE
2", 3 ½", 5", 6 ¼", 7" SIZES
TOOLED, APPLIED and FLAIRED TOPS
COMMON in AMBER
COMMON in the 5" SIZE with a TOOLED TOP, BLUE
RARE in the LARGER SIZES with a TOOLED TOP
ALL APPLIED TOPS are RARE
ALL FLAIRED TOPS are RARE
2" SAMPLE SIZE is SCARCE
COBALT, 6 ¼", A.T., $550.00- 2007
COBALT, 5", A.T., $400.00- 2007
SAPPHIRE BLUE, 5", A.T., $900.00- 2017
COBALT, FLAIR TOP, 5", $300.00- 2017
Note: H.P. WAKELEE TRADE MARKED THE TWO
      LABELS BELOW in 1878. ONE WAS FOR
      A CAMELLINE POWDER in a ROUND
      CONTAINER.

Front: WOODWARD, CLARKE & CO. / CHEMISTS / PORTLAND, OR.

RECT., SMOOTH BASE, 5" and 2 ½"
TOOLED TOP
MILK GLASS and COBALT
RARE

Front: WOODWARD, CLARKE & CO. / PHARMACISTS / PORTLAND, OR.

RECT., SMOOTH BASE, 5"
TOOLED TOP
AMBER
RARE

Front: WISDOM'S / ROBERTINE

RECT., SMOOTH BASE, 5"
FLAT and PANELED FRONTS
TOOLED TOP
COBALT
COMMON
CIRCA: 1888
Locale: PORTLAND, ORE.

EXTRACT TYPE BOTTLES

Front: J.A. BAUER
Side: CHEMIST
Side: SAN FRANCISCO

   RECT., SMOOTH BASE, 5 ½"
   TOOLED TOP
   AQUA
   EX. RARE

Front: DR. CROCKWELL & SON / SALT
       LAKE CITY, UTAH

   RECT., SMOOTH BASE, 5 ½"
   APPLIED TOP
   AQUA
   RARE

Front: M. H. DIGNAN / CHEMIST / SANTA
       ROSA, CAL.

   RECT., SMOOTH BASE, 6 ½"
   TOOLED TOP
   AQUA
   RARE

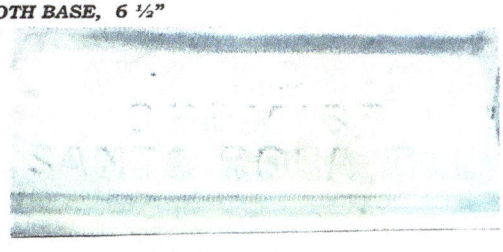

Front: A.A. ENQUIST
Re: CALIFORNIA / WASHING / EXTRACT

   OVAL, SMOOTH BASE, 4 ½"
   FLAIRED TOOLED TOP
   CLEAR FLINT GLASS
   EX. RARE
   Note: AD CIRCA 1865.

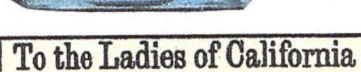

To the Ladies of California

IT IS A FACT, WHICH IT IS important that all should know, that

Washing may be done for half the cost,

And in half the time, required by pursuing the method now in use. An enormous waste of time and materials attends the old and ordinary process. And this is not because a better method is not known, but because housewives persist in treading in the beaten track followed by their mothers and grandmothers before them, opposing every change, and refusing even TO MAKE A FAIR TRIAL of those new inventions which scientific research has produced.

If the housekeepers of San Francisco and of the State will try the

CALIFORNIA WASHING EXTRACT

Simply by way of experiment, they will be amazed to find how much unnecessary labor may be saved by its use. It may be obtained at all the principal Groceries of the city, or in quantities of the Agents, HOSTETTER, SMITH & DEAN.

The use of the EXTRACT renders "rubbing," "pounding," "washboards," and all the severe drudgery of the usual method quite unnecessary. It thoroughly cleanses, without injuring the clothes. In short, it works such wonders as no one will credit without witnessing them. All that the inventor asks of any doubting housewife is

A SINGLE TRIAL.

The following certificate from the State Assayer, furnished after an analysis of the EXTRACT, speaks for itself:

        SAN FRANCISCO, Sept. 19, 1865.
A. A. ENQUIST.
  DEAR SIR:—I have examined the sample of liquid handed me, and find it free from acid or any substance that would be injurious to clothing.
        Very respectfully,
           B. B. THAYER.
☞ **Full Directions** accompany each Bottle.
                se29tf

Side: FRESE'S
Side: EXTRACTS

   RECT., SMOOTH BASE, 4 ½"
   TOOLED TOP
   LT. YELLOW, AQUA, CLEAR
   RARE

Front: FRIZELLE BROS. / MANUF'G /
        CHEMISTS / SAN FRANCISCO, CAL.

   RECT., SMOOTH BASE, 9 ¼"
   APPLIED TOP
   AQUA
   RARE

Side: GATES
Side: SACRAMENTO

   RECT., SMOOTH BASE, 4 ½"
   TOOLED TOP
   CLEAR, AQUA, LT. YELLOW,
     and AMETHYST
   SCARCE

Front: JUSTIN GATES /
        MANUFACTURING /
        CHEMIST /
        SACRAMENTO

   RECT., SMOOTH BASE, 7"
   TOOLED TOP
   AQUA
   RARE
   Note: AD FROM S.F. and SACRAMENTO
        IS CIRCA 1874

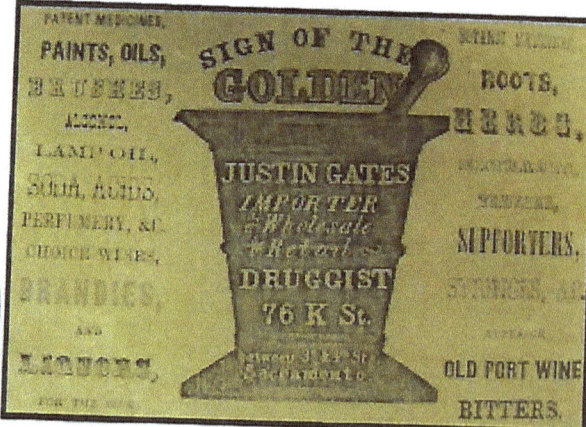

Front: DOUBLE / CONCENTRATED /
        EXTRACTS
Side: GUITTARD & CO.
Side: SAN FRANCISCO

   RECT., SMOOTH BASE, 5 ¼:
   TOOLED TOP
   CLEAR
   RARE

Front: F.M. HILBY / MONTEREY, CAL.

   RECT., SMOOTH BASE, 6 ¾"
   TOOLED TOP
   SCARCE
   AQUA, $130.00- 2017

Front: "monogram" / HESPERIAN / CHEMICAL / ASSOCIATION

   RECT., SMOOTH BASE, 8"
   TOOLED TOP
   CLEAR
   SCARCE
   CIRCA: 1900
   Locale: WASHINGTON

Front: "monogram" / HESPERIAN / CHEMICAL / ASSOCIATION

   RECT., SMOOTH BASE, 5 ½"
   TOOLED TOP
   AQUA and CLEAR
   SCARCE
   CIRCA: 1895-1905
   Locale: WASHINGTON

Front: "monogram" / HESPERIAN / CHEMICAL / ASSOCIATION

   RECT., SMOOTH BASE, 6"
   TOOLED TOP
   CLEAR
   SCARCE
   CIRCA: 1898-1903
   Locale: WASHINGTON

Side: C. LANGLEY & CO.
Front: WHOLESALE DRUGGISTS
        SAN FRANCISCO
Side: CALIFORNIA

   RECT., SMOOTH BASE, 4 ½"
   TOOLED TOP
   AQUA
   RARE

Front: C. LANGLEY / SAN FRANCISCO

   RECT., SMOOTH BASE, 4 ½"
   APPLIED and TOOLED TOP
   AQUA, CLEAR FLINT GLASS
   COMMON

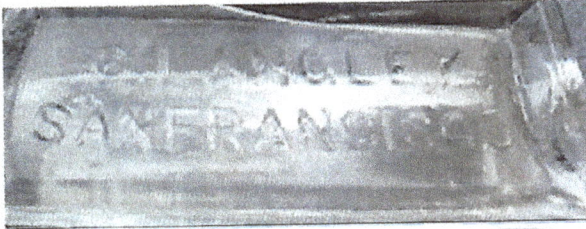

Front: H. LEVI & CO. / WHOLESALE GROCERS / SAN FRANCISCO

   RECT., SMOOTH BASE, 6"
   TOOLED TOP
   CLEAR
   SCARCE

Front: **LOW'S / EXTRACTS**

    RECT., SMOOTH BASE, 4 ¾"
    FLAIRED TOP
    CLEAR and LT. AQUA
    SCARCE
    CIRCA: 1867
    Note: SHEPARDSON and GATES WERE THE
       AGENTS FOR THIS BRAND IN S.F.
       THIS BOTTLE HAS BEEN SEEN DAMAGED in a
       LARGER SIZE. THESE WOULD BE EX. RARE.

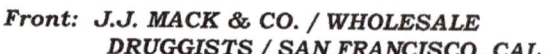

Front: **J.J. MACK & CO. / WHOLESALE DRUGGISTS / SAN FRANCISCO, CAL.**

    RECT., SMOOTH BASE, 5"
    TOOLED TOP
    AQUA and CLEAR
    SCARCE

Front: **C.J. PETERS / SACRAMENTO, CAL.**

    RECT.,, SMOOTH BASE, 8 ½"
    TOOLED TOP
    AQUA
    SCARCE

Side: **REDINGTON'S**
Side: **EXTRACTS**

    RECT., SMOOTH BASE, 4 ½"
    TOOLED TOP
    CLEAR and AQUA
    COMMON

Front: **PAUL RIEGER'S / FLAVORING EXTRACTS / SAN FRANCISCO**

    RECT., SMOOTH BASE, 5"
    TOOLED TOP
    AQUA
    COMMON

Front: **PAUL RIEGER & CO. / SAN FRANCISCO, CAL.**

    SQUARE, SMOOTH BASE, 9 ½"
    TOOLED TOP
    AQUA
    SCARCE

Side: RHODES & CO.
Side: SAN JOSE

    RECT., SMOOTH BASE, 7"
    TOOLED TOP
    AQUA
    RARE

Side: SMITH & DAVIS
Side: PORTLAND, O.

    RECT., SMOOTH BASE, 4 ½"
    FLAIRED TOP
    AQUA
    EX. RARE

Front: J.J. SPIEKER
Side: SACRAMENTO
Side: N.W. COR. 6th & K STS.

    RECT., SMOOTH BASE, 5 ¾"
    APPLIED TOP
    AQUA and LIME GREEN
    RARE

Front: B.B. THAYER / & CO. / SAN FRANCISCO
Side: CHEMIST
Side: DRUGGIST

    RECT., SMOOTH BASE, 4"
    FLAIRED TOP
    CLEAR FLINT GLASS
    EX. RARE

Front: monogram / WRIGHT & BROWN / DRUGGISTS /
       HEALDSBURG, CAL.

    RECT., SMOOTH BASE, 5 ¼"
    TOOLED TOP
    CLEAR
    RARE

Side: HUG'S
Side: EXTRACTS

    RECT., SMOOTH BASE, 5"
    TOOLED TOP
    CLEAR
    RARE

FLORIDA WATER, BAY RUM & TOILET WATER TYPE BOTTLES

Front: C & B *(embossed in indented panel)*

    ROUND, SMOOTH BASE, 2 ½"
    APPLIED TOP
    EX. RARE

Front: C & B / S.F. *(embossed in indented panel)*

    ROUND, SMOOTH BASE, 6 ¼"
    APPLIED and TOOLED TOP
    DEEP AQUA
    SCARCE

Front: CRANE & BRIGHAM / SAN FRANCISCO
    (embossed in indented panel)

    ROUND, SMOOTH BASE, 9 ¼"
    APPLIED TOP
    AQUA
    COMMON
    Note: HAS WESTERN CURVED R's
    Note: AT RIGHT is an AD FROM THE 1874
        S.F. DIRECTORY.

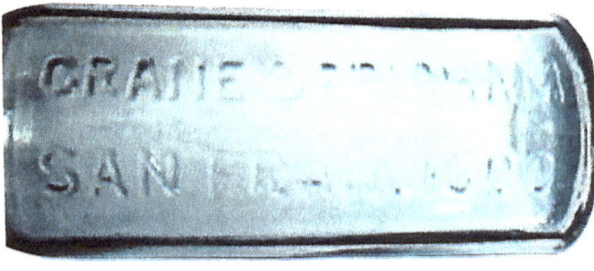

Front: CRANE & BRIGHAM / SAN FRANCISCO
    (embossed in a leaf motif)

    ROUND, BAY RUM SHAPE, SMOOTH BASE
    APPLIED RING TOP, 10 ¼" and 14"
    RARE in BOTH SIZES
    YELLOW AMBER, 14", $900.00- 2017
    AMBER, 10 ¼", $650.00- 2014
    Note: HAS WESTERN CURVED R's

Front: CRANE & / BRIGHAM S.F.
Re: motif of VINES

    RECT., with CONCAVE EDGES
    TOOLED TOP
    5 ¼", 6 ½" and 8 ½"
    AQUA
    CLEAR, 5 ¼", $50.00- 2006
    ALL SIZES are SCARCE

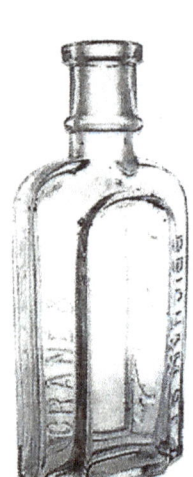

Front: **FLORIDA WATER / COFFIN – REDINGTON CO. / SAN FRANCISCO**

    ROUND, SMOOTH BASE, 8 ¾"
    TOOLED TOP
    AQUA
    COMMON

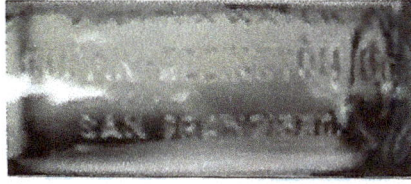

Front: **FLORIDA WATER / DAVIS BRO'S / SAN FRANCISCO**

    ROUND, SMOOTH BASE, 9 ¼"
    APPLIED TOP
    AQUA
    SCARCE

Front: **WM. GOLDSTEIN'S / IXL / FLORIDA WATER**

    ROUND, SMOOTH BASE, 9"
    APPLIED TOP
    SCARCE
    AQUA, $40.00- 2017

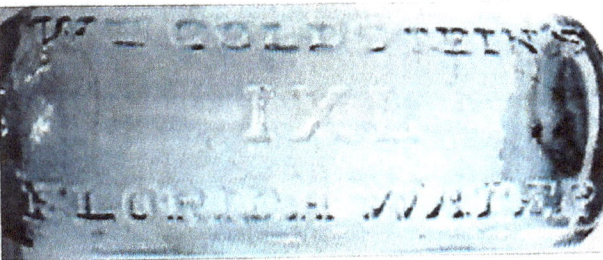

Front: **MACK'S / FLORIDA WATER**

    ROUND, SMOOTH BASE, 6" and 9"
    TOOLED TOP
    AQUA
    SCARCE
    Note: BILLHEAD BELOW is FROM 1897.

Front: H.A. PERFUME CO. / bell / TRADE MARK /
SAN FRANCISCO / SHANGHAI

    ROUND, SMOOTH BASE, 6" and 9"
    TOOLED TOP
    AQUA
    SCARCE

Front: PERFECTION / FLORIDA WATER / L.DI.N.S.F.

    ROUND, SMOOTH BASE, 9"
    APPLIED TOP
    AQUA
    RARE
    Note: NO PIC AVAILABLE

Front: LANGLEY & MICHAELS S.F. (in plate)
Re: motif of VINES

    RECT., CONCAVE EDGES
    5 ¼:, 6 ½", and 8 ½"
    TOOLED TOP
    AQUA
    RARE

Front: LANGLEY & MICHAELS / SAN FRANCISCO
    (embossed in rect. or indented plate)

    ROUND, SMOOTH BASE, 6" and 9"
    TOOLED TOP
    COMMON in AQUA
    RARE in LIME GREEN
    Note: BILLHEAD BELOW is FROM 1898.

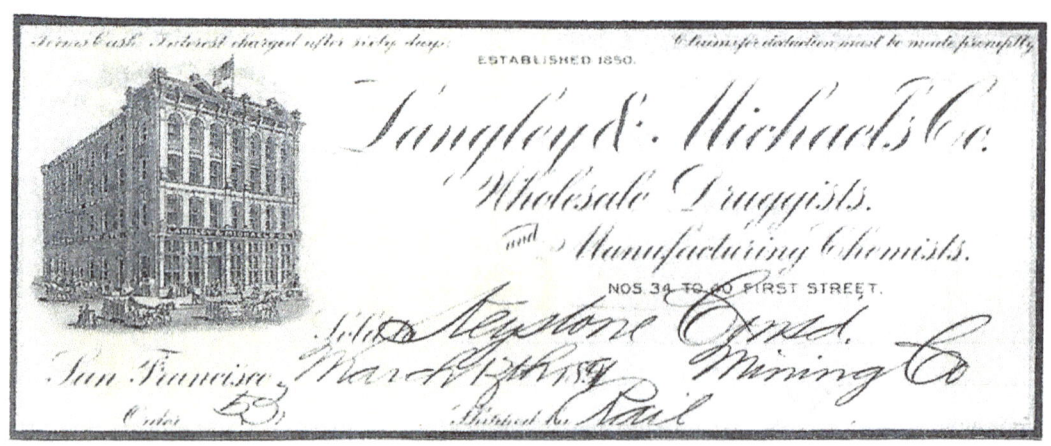

Front: MACK'S / BRIGHTON / COLOGNE / MACK & CO. / PROPRIETORS / SAN FRANCISCO

ROUND, SMOOTH BASE
6 ¾" and 9"
TOOLED TOP
AQUA
EX. RARE

FURNITURE REVIVER.

Front: FLORIDA WATER / MERTEN, MOFFIT & CO. / SAN FRANCISCO
(in rect. plate)

ROUND, SMOOTH BASE, 9"
TOOLED TOP
AQUA
SCARCE
Note: RARE TRADE CARDS FROM MERTEN and MOFFITT AT THE RIGHT. I BELIEVE THESE WERE DISTRIBUTED AS A SET.
CIRCA 1890's

Front: **FLORIDA WATER / REDINGTON & CO. / SAN FRANCISCO**

ROUND, SMOOTH BASE
6" and 9"
TOOLED TOP
AQUA
COMMON
Note: CIRCA 1890's TRADE CARD at RIGHT

Front: **AQUA DE FLORIDA / DE COCHEU / REDINGTON & CO. / SAN FRANCISCO**

ROUND, SMOOTH BASE, 9"
APPLIED TOP
AQUA
RARE

Front: **REDINGTON & CO. / monogram / SAN FRANCISCO**

ROUND BAY RUM SHAPE, 10 ¼"
SMOOTH BASE
APPLIED RING TOP
RARE
AMBER, $130.00 - 2017
Note: HAS WESTERN CURVED R's
Note: BELOW is a 1881 BILLHEAD.

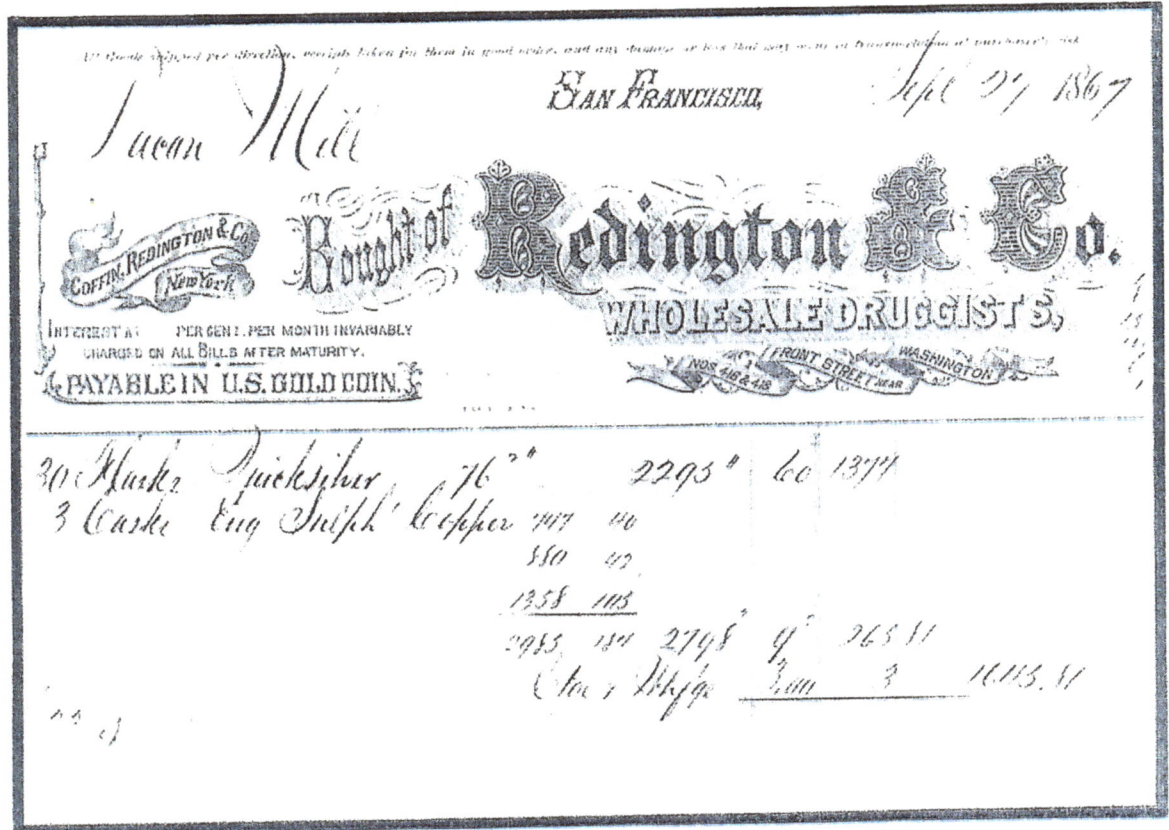

Front: REDINGTON & CO. /
fancy design /
SAN FRANCISCO

ROUND, SMOOTH BASE
TOOLED TOP, 7 ½"
LT. AMBER
EX. RARE
Note: LOOKS LIKE A COLGATE
COLOGNE BOTTLE and
IS VERY LIGHTLY
EMBOSSED.
Note: AD at RIGHT IS CIRCA
1866. BILLHEAD AT
the TOP IS CIRCA
1867 AND MADE OUT
TO THE BACON MILL
ON THE CARSON RIVER.

Front: **SEARBY'S / FLORIDA WATER**

    ROUND, SMOOTH BASE, 9"
    APPLIED TOP
    AQUA
    SCARCE
    Note: AD at RIGHT is
          CIRCA 1878

Front: **JAMES G. STEELE & CO. / EXTRA COLOGNE / (mortar & pestle) / SAN FRANCISCO / CAL.**

    ROUND, SMOOTH BASE, 7 ½"
    TOOLED TOP
    AQUA
    EX. RARE

Front: **FLORIDA WATER / WEM / SAN FRANCISCO**
        (in indented panel)

    ROUND, SMOOTH BASE, 9"
    APPLIED TOP
    SCARCE
    AQUA, $40.00 - 2017
    Note: HAS WESTERN CURVED R's

Front: **S. W.E.M. (in circle) F.**
        (in indented panel)

    ROUND, SMOOTH BASE, 6 ¾"
    APPLIED TOP
    AQUA
    RARE

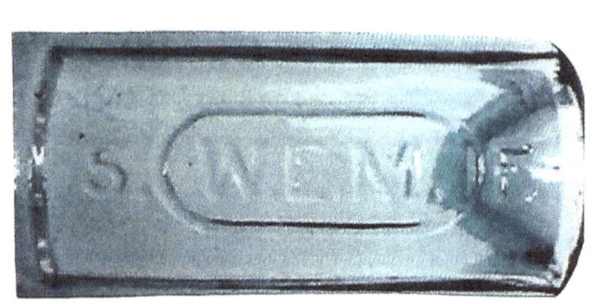

Front: FLORIDA WATER / WESTERN PERFUMERY CO. / SAN FRANCISCO

ROUND, SMOOTH BASE, 6 ½" and 9"
TOOLED TOP
AQUA
RARE in BOTH SIZES
Note: THIS LABEL WAS TRADE MARKED in 1884 by LOUIS GREENBAUM in SAN FRANCISCO. FANCY TRADE CARD is CIRCA 1890's.

Front: **W.E.M.** *(in oval plate)* / **S.F.**
    (all in indented panel)

ROUND, SMOOTH BASE, 9" *(if whole)*
APPLIED TOP
YELLOW GREEN
EX. RARE

Toys, Baskets, Fancy Goods, etc., at Thurnauer & Zinn's, 219 Battery st., S. F.

192   DIRECTORY OF CENTRAL PACIFIC R. R.

Reilay J. P., physician, Odd Fellows' Bldg., Marysville.
Reilly J. J., stereoscopic views, 183 El Dorado, Stockt'n.
REILLY P. J., druggist, Broadway, near 7th, Oakland.
Reiser E., wagon maker, Red Bluff.
Reiser L. A., harness and saddles, 6 Main, Chico.
Relyea S. B., carriage trimmer, cor 13th and J, Sac'to.
Renner Maurice, saloon, Yreka.
REPUBLICAN PUBLISHING CO., prop'r San Joaquin *Republican*, 226 Main, Stockton.
Reud W. R., physician, cor. J and 5th. Sacramento.
Renfu Rev. L. C., clergyman, M. E. S., res. Aurora, Stockton.
REYNOLDS H. H., Cashier San Jose Sav. Bank, 308 First, San Jose.
Reynolds Mrs. R. T., millinery, Broadway, bet. 5th and 6th, Oakland.
Rhoades A. L., Judge Supreme Court, Sacramento.
Rhoades & Hornblower, saloon, 2d, bet. J and K, Sacramento.
Rhodes, Arnold & Co., prop'rs Woodland Mills, 87 Front, Sacramento.
Rhodes, Eves & Co., prop'rs Eagle Mills, 87 Front, Sacramento.
Rice Charles, prop'r Iowa Hill Stage Line, Colfax.

P. J. REILLY, M. D.
DRUGGIST,
Dealer in
FINE DRUGS, MEDICINES, CHEMICALS, PERFUMERY,
Fancy Goods, Patent Medicines, Etc.

BROADWAY,
One door below Seventh Street,   OAKLAND.

H. S. Crocker & Co., Printers and Stationers, Sacramento and S. F.

HAIR BOTTLES

Front: COLLINS / HAIR GROWER / & DANDRUFF SPECIFIC /
W.R. COLLINS, S.F.

    RECT., SMOOTH BASE, 7 ¾"
    TOOLED TOP
    RARE
    AQUA, $60.00- 2019
    CIRCA: 1895

Front: EUREKA / HAIR / RESTORATIVE
Side: P.J. REILLY
Side: SAN FARNCISCO

    RECT., SMOOTH BASE, 7 ½"
    APPLIED and TOOLED TOP
    RARE
    AQUA with APPLIED TOP, $475.00- 2017
    CIRCA: 1868
    Note: EASTERN BLOWN VARIENT HAS
          A TOOLED TOP AND IS USUALLY
          PALE AQUA, $450.00- 2006
    Note: AD at LOWER RIGHT is FROM
          THE 1867 S.F. DIRECTORY.

EASTERN BLOWN VARIENT SHOWN BELOW

Front: FOUNTAIN OF YOUTH / HAIR RESTORER

    RECT., SMOOTH BASE, 7 ½"
    TOOLED TOP
    RARE
    COBALT, $700.00- 2015
    Locale: SACRAMENTO, CAL.

Front: **FISH'S INFALLIABLE / HAIR RESTORATIVE**
(embossed vertically)
Shoulder: **N. MILLS**

ROUND, SMOOTH BASE, 7 ½"
APPLIED TOP
COBALT, $3000.00- 2009
Locale: SAN FRANCISCO, CAL.
Note: ALL ADS are FROM S.F. DIRECTORYS.

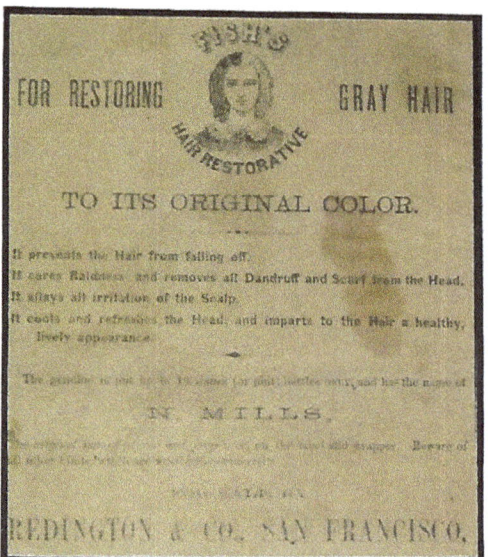

CIRCA 1863 AD

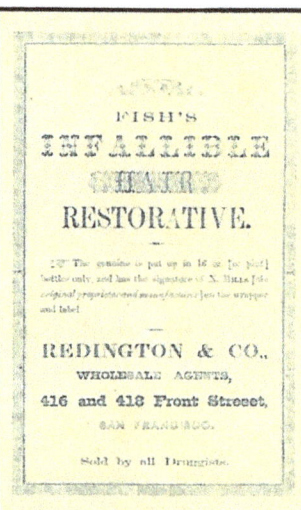

LABEL TRADE MARKED in 1863
by REDINGTON & CO. in S.F.

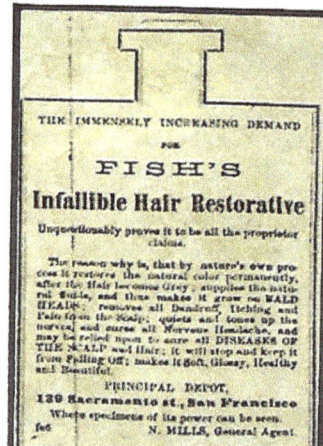

CIRCA 1863 AD

CIRCA 1858 AD

CIRCA 1862 AD

FIRST LABEL TRADE MARKED in
1863 by CHAS. STORY in S.F.

Front: FISH'S / HAIR RESTORATIVE
Side: B.F. FISH
Side: SAN FRANCISCO

    RECT., SMOOTH BASE, 7 ¼"
    APPLIED TOP
    RARE
    AQUA, $450.00- 2009
    CLEAR FLINT GLASS, $725.00- 1996
    Note: THE LABEL ABOVE RIGHT WAS
    TRADE MARKED in 1863 by
    B.F. FISH and NORMAN COON
    in SAN FRANCISCO.

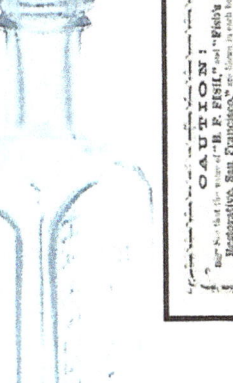

Side: I. FORBES & CO.
Side: E. H. R.

    RECT., SMOOTH BASE, 7 ½"
    TOOLED TOP
    AQUA
    EX. RARE
    Locale: OGDEN, UTAH, with AGENTS in S.F.,
    MARYSVILLE and WASH. STATE. THIS was
    "ENGINEER'S HAIR REMEDY". I HAVE SEEN
    ADS FOR THIS PRODUCT FROM the LATE 1890'S.

Side: A. GRIMM'S
Front: REJUVENATOR / FOR THE HAIR
Side: SAN FRANCISCO

    RECT., SMOOTH BASE, 6 ¾"
    APPLIED TOP
    AQUA
    EX. RARE
    CIRCA: 1870

Side: J.R. LIPMAN
Side: SAN FRANCISCO

    RECT., SMOOTH BASE, 6 ½"
    APPLIED and TOOLED TOP
    AQUA, APPLIED TOP, $30.00- 2017
    SCARCE
    Note: AD FROM THE NAPA REGISTER, AUG 3, 1872.

Front: INDIAN QUEEN
Side: HENLEY'S
Side: HAIR RESTORATIVE

   RECT., SMOOTH BASE, 7 ½"
   APPLIED TOP
   SHADES of BLUE, GREEN and AQUA
   BLUE, $1000.00- 2009 (crack)

Front: T. JONES / CORAL
Re: HAIR / RESTORATIVE

   RECT., OPEN PONTIL, 5"
   APPLIED TOP
   AQUA
   EX. RARE
   Locale: SAN FRANCISCO
   Note: AD FROM the 1858 SAN
         FRANCISCO DIRECTORY.

Front: LUXOR / HAIR STIMULATOR &
       DANDRUFF ERADICATOR
Re: BLUMAUDER – FRANK DRUG CO. /
       MANUFACTURERS /
       PORTLAND, OREGON

   RECT., SMOOTH BASE, 7 ½"
   TOOLED TOP
   CLEAR
   RARE

Front: DR. MATHEW'S / GRAY HAIR / RESTORER /
       SAN FRANCISCO

   RECT., SMOOTH BASE, 7"
   TOOLED TOP
   SCARCE
   CLEAR, $200.00- 2017

Front: **DR. E.E. McLEAN'S / MEDICATED / HAIR TONIC / SAN FRANCISCO**

RECT., SMOOTH BASE, 6"
TOOLED TOP
SCARCE
LT. AMETHYST, $40.00- 2017

Front: **J.A. McCORMICK'S / HAIR DYE / SAN FRANCISCO, CAL.**

RECT., SMOOTH BASE, 5 ¾"
TOOLED TOP
CLEAR
SCARCE

Front: **MRS. / M.A. RAGSDALE & CO.**

RECT., SMOOTH BASE, 6 ¾"
APPLIED TOP
AQUA
EX. RARE, POSSIBLY UNIQUE
Note: THIS BOTTLE WAS DUG in S.F. AND HAS THE APPEARANCE of a WESTERN BLOWN BOTTLE.

Front: **M.A. REAVES / GREAT ELECTRIC / HAIR TONIC**

RECT., SMOOTH BASE, 6 ½"
APPLIED and TOOLED TOP
AQUA, TOOLED TOP, $140.00- 2017
RARE with APPLIED TOP
SCARCE with TOOLED TOP
Note: HAS THE WESTERN CURVED R's.
Note: AD BELOW IS FROM THE 1882 S.F. DIRECTORY.

Front: THE GREAT / HAIR / PRODUCER
Side: PROF. J.R. TILTON
Side: S.F. CAL.
Re: THE / CROWN OF / SCIENCE

    RECT., SMOOTH BASE, 7"
    APPLIED TOP
    RARE
    SAPPHIRE BLUE, $1000.00- 2017
    Note: HAS WESTERN CURVED R's
    Note: AD BELOW is CIRCA 1877.

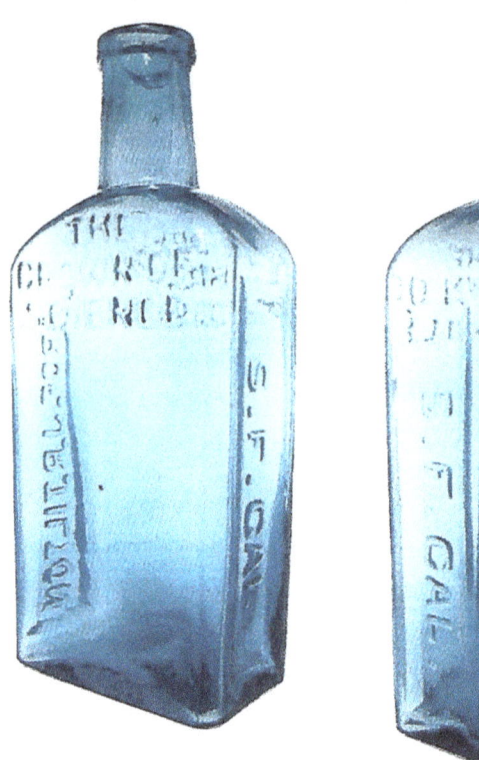
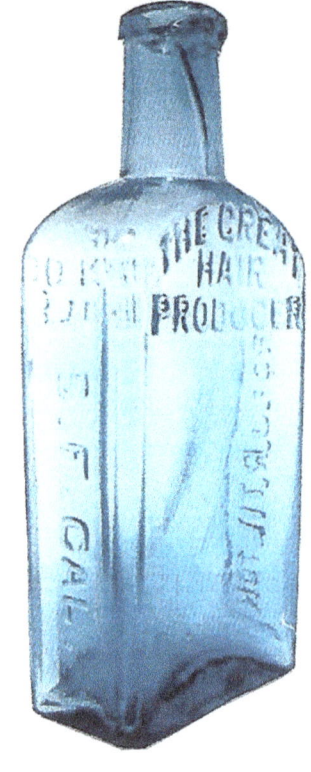

Front: ST. CLAIR'S / HAIR LOTION

    RECT., SMOOTH BASE, 7 ¼" and 8"
    TOOLED and APPLIED TOP
    COBALT, 7 ¼", T.T., $300.00- 2011
    COBALT, 8", T.T., $450.00- 2009
    COMMON in the 7 14" SIZE with T.T.
    EX. RARE in the 8" SIZE
    APPLIED TOP VARIENT is WESTERN
      BLOWN and is EX. RARE. SHOWN at
      NEAR RIGHT.
  Note: TRADE MARKED in 1871 by
    H. BOWMAN, SACRAMENTO. AD ABOVE
    RIGHT is CIRCA 1872.

Side: TWIABA
Side: WARRANTED

RECT., SMOOTH BASE, 7"
APPLIED TOP
BLUE AQUA, $750.00- 1996
EX. RARE
Locale: ELKO, NEVADA
Note: THE DAILY ALTA CALIFORNIA RAN THE FIRST AD FOR THIS PROCUCT ON MAY 6, 1871. SEE BELOW. ON NOV. 16, 1871 ANOTHER AD APPEARED LISTING CHAS. E. HINCKLEY AS THE AGENT IN S.F. THE SACRAMENTO DAILY UNION RAN AN AD ON MAY 3, 1873, LISTING TERRY McMORRY AS THE AGENT FOR SACRAMENTO. SEE BOTTOM RIGHT. BOTTLES WERE NO DOUBT BLOWN IN SAN FRANCISCO, PROBABLY BETWEEN 1871 and 1873.

TWIABA—TO THE BALD HEADED— NEVADA NATURAL HAIR RESTORATIVE OF WHITE SAGE. Don't fail to use the above preparation and beBald no more. J. B. FITCH & CO., Proprietors, Elko, Nevada. The Restorative is scientifically compounded, principally from purely Vegetable matter, gathered from the mountains and plains of Nevada, and contains no ingredient that is not in itself of a Restoring, Cleansing and Purifying character. We do not claim and do not believe that White Sage, simply steeped or boiled to a tea, will restore the hair; but we do claim and also know that our PREPARATION of White Sage is a sure cure for baldness. To restore the hair to the human head in cases of baldness it has no equal. As a speedy cure for Dandruff er any disease of the head or scalp, our Preparation of White Sage is unsurpassed. Is a sure preventive of the hair becoming gray, and by constant application will restore gray hair to its original color, beauty and strength. As a dressing for the hair and an article for the Toilet Table, it is unrivaled. Beware of counterfeits, as none is genuine unless bearing the date of our Letters Patent, issued March 14th, 1871, and prepared by JOSEPH F. BOARDMAN & CO., Elko, Nevada. Price, $1 50 per bottle; $15 per doz: $8 per half doz. Address all communications to JOSEPH F. BOARDMAN, Superintendent White Sage Manufactory, Elko, Nevada. my4

"TWIABA,"
OR
NEVADA WHITE SAGE
Hair Restorative.

THE ONLY SURE RESTORER OF THE HAIR AND PROMOTER OF ITS GROWTH.
For sale by the Agent.

CHAS. E. HINCKLEY,
Chemist and Apothecary,
32 POST STREET.

See the name "TWIABA" on each bottle and take no other. no26-2p

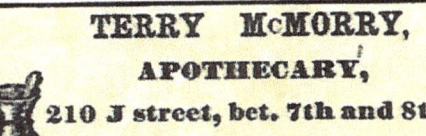

TERRY McMORRY,
APOTHECARY,
210 J street, bet. 7th and 8th.
PURE DRUGS AND CHEMICALS.
Choice Perfumery and Toilet Articles.
Pure Wines and Liquors for medicinal purposes.
Agent for "TWIABA," White Sage Hair Restorative. j2-1m1p

JAMAICA GINGER BOTTLES

Front: ABRAMS & CARROLL / ESS OF / JAMAICA GINGER / SAN FRANCISCO

OVAL, SMOOTH BASE
APPLIED TOP
AQUA
EX. RARE
Note: AD is CIRCA 1878. THIS BOTTLE has 2 TYPES of FONTS. TAPERED TOP VERSION has the CURVED WESTERN R's.

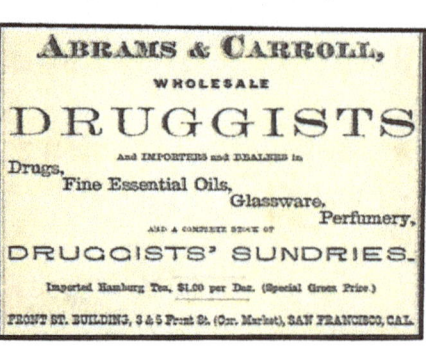

Front: ADDOMS & GLOVER / CONCENTRATED / ESSENCE OF / JAMAICA GINGER

OVAL, SMOOTH BASE
APPLIED TOP
AQUA
EX. RARE
Locale: CHEYENNE. WYO.

Front: ADDOMS & GLOVER / CHEYENNE / W.T.

OVAL, SMOOTH BASE
APPLIED TOP
AQUA
EX. RARE

Front: ALLEN'S / ESSENCE OF / JAMAICA GINGER

OVAL, SMOOTH BASE
APPLIED TOP
AQUA
EX. RARE
Circa: 1867
Locale: SACRAMENTO
Note: ALLEN MOVED TO S.F. IN 1873.
AD CIRCA 1871.

Front: DR. BARNES / ESS JAMAICA GINGER / R. HALL & CO. / PROPRIETORS

OVAL, SMOOTH BASE
APPLIED TOP
SCARCE in AQUA
EX. RARE in SAPPHIRE BLUE and CLEAR
RARE in GREEN
Locale: SAN FRANCISCO, CA.

Front: DR. BARNES / ESS JAMAICA GINGER /
J.R. GATES & CO. / PROPRIETORS

OVAL, SMOOTH BASE
APPLIED and TOOLED TOP
SCARCE in AQUA
EX. RARE in CLEAR and YELLOW TINT
Circa: 1880
Locale: SAN FRANCISCO, CAL.
Note" AD CIRCA 1888

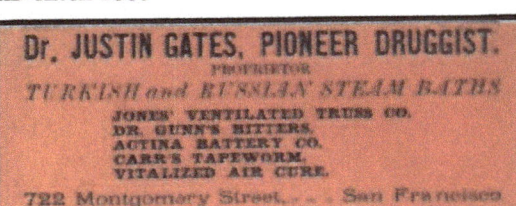

Front: DR. BARNES / ESS JAMAICA GINGER /
SHEPARDSON & GATES / PROPRIETORS

OVAL, SMOOTH BASE
APPLIED and TOOLED TOP
AQUA
RARE
Circa: 1867
Locale: SAN FRANCISCO, CAL.
Note: AD CIRCA 1867

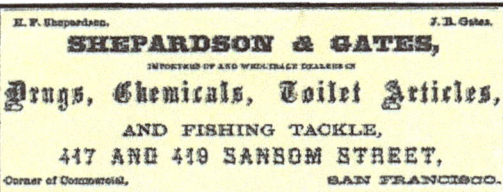

Front: BOTHIN MANF'G / SAN FRANCISCO, CA.

OVAL, SMOOTH BASE
TOOLED TOP
AQUA
SCARCE

Front: DR. COLLIS BROWN'S / ESS OF JAMAICA
GINGER / NO. 55 HAYMARKET ST. /
LONDON

OVAL, SMOOTH BASE
APPLIED and TOOLED TOP
SCARCE in AQUA and CLEAR
RARE in GREEN
Note: APPLIED TOP VARIENTS APPEAR TO BE
WESTERN BLOWN

Front: CRANE & BRIGHAM / WHOLESALE
DRUGGISTS / SAN FRANCISCO
(in indented panel)

OVAL, SMOOTH BASE
APPLIED TOP
AQUA, CLEAR and LT. PURPLE
SCARCE
Circa: 1868
Note: HAS WESTERN CURVED R's

Front: **CRANE & BRIGHAM / SAN FRANCISCO**
  (in indented panel)

  OVAL, SMOOTH BASE
  APPLIED and TOOLED TOP
  AQUA
  SCARCE
  Note: HAS WESTERN CURVED R's

Front: **J.A. FOLGER & CO. / ESSENCE OF / JAMAICA GINGER / SAN FRANCISCO**

  OVAL, SMOOTH BASE
  TOOLED TOP
  AQUA
  COMMON

Front: **E. FREESE / S.F.**

  OVAL, SMOOTH BASE
  APPLIED, TOOLED and FLAIRED TOP
  SCARCE in AQUA
  EX. RARE in COLORS
  CLEAR FLINT GLASS, $190.00- 2005
  AMETHYST
  LIME GREEN
  BLUE
  Note: THERE ARE MANY DIFFERENT SHAPES
     OF OVALS AND TOP COMBINATIONS
     FOR THIS BOTTLE. SOME HAVE THE
     WESTERN CURVED R's AND OTHERS
     APPEAR TO BE EASTERN BLOWN.

Front: **GODBE & CO'S / ESS OF / JAMAICA GINGER / SALT LAKE CITY**

  OVAL, SMOOTH BASE
  APPLIED and TOOLED TOP
  AQUA
  SCARCE
  Varient: misspelled "JAMICA"
  Note: THERE ARE A FEW DIFFERENT
     EMBOSSING PATTERNS FOR THIS
     BRAND.

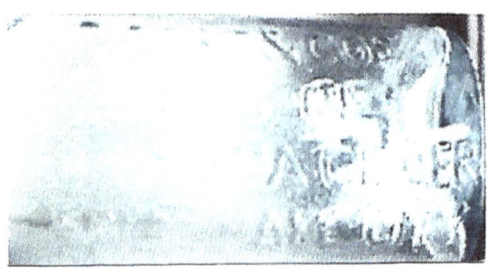

Front: HALL'S / ESS OF / JAMAICA GINGER

OVAL, SMOOTH BASE
TOOLED TOP
AQUA
RARE
Locale: SAN FRANCISCO
Note: I BELIEVE THESE to be EASTERN BLOWN

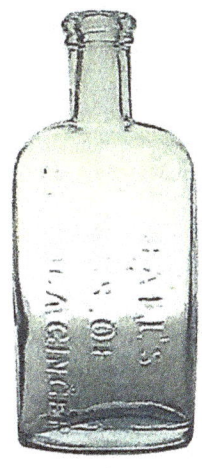

Front: HOSTETTER'S / ESSENCE / JAMAICA GINGER / PITTSBURG

OVAL, SMOOTH BASE
APPLIED, TOOLED and FLAIRED TOP
COMMON in AQUA
RARE in COLORS
FLAIRED TOP VARIENTS are also RARE
Note: HAS WESTERN CURVED R's

CIRCA 1868 AD FOR LACOUR'S JAMAICA GINGER. THIS IS THE SAME LOUIS LACOUR OF BITTERS FAME. SO FAR NO EMBOSSED BOTTLE HAS TURNED UP FOR THIS BRAND.

Front: HURLBUT BROTHERS / CHEYENNE / W.T.

OVAL, SMOOTH BASE
APPLIED TOP
AQUA
EX. RARE

Front: **LANGLEY & MICHAELS / ESS / JAMAICA GINGER**

    OVAL, SMOOTH BASE
    TOOLED TOP
    AQUA
    SCARCE
    Locale: SAN FRANCISCO, CAL.

Front: **LANGLEY'S / ESS / JAMAICA GINGER / SAN FRANCISCO**

    OVAL, SMOOTH BASE
    APPLIED and TOOLED TOP
    CLEAR FLINT GLASS, SCARCE
    AQUA, SCARCE
    GREEN, EX. RARE

Front: **E.G. LYONS & CO. / ESS / JAMAICA GINGER / S.F.**

    OVAL, SMOOTH BASE
    APPLIED and TOOLED TOP
    COMMON in AQUA
    EX. RARE in GREEN, AMETHYST and LT. BLUE
    Note: AD AT BOTTOM RIGHT IS FROM THE 1874 S.F. DIRECTORY.

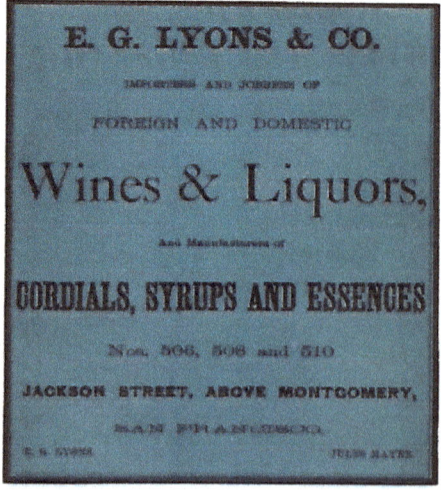

Front: **MERTEN MFG. / S.F. CAL.**

    OVAL, SMOOTH BASE
    TOOLED TOP
    RARE in LIME GREEN
    COMMON in AQUA
    CIRCA: 1890
    Note: EXTRACT LABEL WAS TRADE MARKED IN 1895.

Front: McMILLAN & KESTER / ESS OF / JAMAICA / GINGER / S.F.

OVAL, IRON PONTIL and SMOOTH BASE
APPLIED and TOOLED TOP
EX. RARE IN LIME GREEN,
 $400.00- 1996
COMMON in AQUA, $30.00- 2002
EX. RARE with IRON PONTIL ,
 $200.00- 1996, AQUA
Note: HAS WESTERN CURVED R's

Front: McMILLAN & KESTER'S / ESS / JAMAICA / GINGER / S.F.

OVAL, SMOOTH BASE
APPLIED TOP
AQUA, $60.00- 1998
GREEN, $150.00- 1996
DEEP GREEN, $100.00- 1997
BLUE, $300.00- 2017 (crack)
COMMON in AQUA
EX. RARE in COLORS

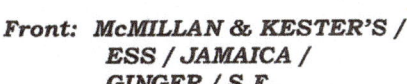

Front: MERTEN, MOFFITT & CO. / SAN FRANCISCO (in rect. plate)

OVAL, SMOOTH BASE
TOOLED TOP
COMMON in AQUA
EX. RARE in LIME GREEN

Front: MITCHELL'S / ESSENCE / JAMAICA GINGER / PITTSBURG

OVAL, SMOOTH BASE
APPLIED and TOOLED TOP
AQUA
SCARCE
Note: BLOWN in the HOSTETTERS MOLD with MITCHELLS SLUGGED IN. HAS THE WESTERN CURVED R's.

Base: **O.G.W.**

    OVAL, SMOOTH BASE
    TOOLED TOP
    AQUA
    EX. RARE
    CIRCA: 1882
    Note: OAKLAND GLASS WORKS

Front: **DONALD McMILLAN / SAN FRANCISCO**

    OVAL, SMOOTH BASE
    TOOLED TOP
    AQUA
    EX. RARE
    Note: DONALD McMILLAN was the SUCESSOR to McMILLAN and KESTER. AD at RIGHT is FROM THE 1882 S.F. DIRECTORY.

Front: **REDINGTON & CO. / ESS OF / JAMAICA GINGER / SAN FRANCISCO**

    OVAL, SMOOTH BASE
    APPLIED and TOOLED TOP
    COMMON in AQUA
    EX. RARE in LIME GREEN
    Note: AD is CIRCA 1867

Front: **PAUL RIEGER'S / JAMAICA GINGER / S.F. CAL.**

    OVAL, SMOOTH BASE
    TOOLED TOP
    COMMON in AQUA
    RARE in GREEN

Front: TURNER'S / ESS OF / JAMAICA GINGER / S.F.

    OVAL, SMOOTH BASE
    APPLIED and TOOLED TOP
    AQUA
    EX. RARE
    Note: THERE IS ALSO A WESTERN BLOWN VARIENT
          OF THE NEW YORK TURNER BROS. BOTTLE.
          IT HAS AN APPLIED TOP AND IS SEEN IN
          AQUA AND SHADES OF GREEN. IT IS EASY
          TO TELL THE DIFFERENCE FROM THE
          EASTERN BLOWN BOTTLE, AS IT IS USUALLY
          CLEAN AND SHINY WITHOUT HAVING TO BE
          TUMBLED OR POLISHED.

Front: W.T. WENZELL / SAN FRANCISCO

    OVAL, SMOOTH BASE
    APPLIED AND TOOLED TOP
    COMMON in AQUA
    EX. RARE in GREEN, $230.00- 1996

Front: **W (in oval plate)**

    OVAL, SMOOTH BASE
    APPLIED TOP
    COMMON in AQUA
    EX. RARE in GREEN and BLUE
    Circa: 1867
    Locale: SAN FRANCISCO, THIS WAS THE
       FIRST BOTTLE USED BY W.T. WENZELL.

Front: **unembossed**

    OVAL, SMOOTH BASE
    TOOLED TOP
    COBALT
    EX. RARE
    Note: JUST HAD TO ADD THIS ONE. IT WAS DUG
       IN THE WEST AND NO DOUBT WESTERN
       BLOWN.

Note: A FEW THINGS ABOUT JAMAICA GINGER BOTTLES. MANY OF THESE BRANDS COME WITH DIFFERENT STYLE TOPS. THEY MAY BE APPPLIED OR TOOLED, DOUBLE COLLAR, SINGLE COLLAR OR FLAIR TOP. SOME HAVE EASTERN BLOWN VARIENTS. THE WESTERN MADE BOTTLES ARE USUALLY MUCH CLEANER WHEN THEY COME OUT OF THE GROUND. THIS IS DUE TO BETTER QUALITY GLASS. HEIGHTS CAN VARY FROM 5" TO OVER 6", SOMETIMES WITH THE SAME BRAND.

PATENT MEDICINE TYPE BOTTLES

Front: ABEL'S WHITE PINE / BALSAM / LOS ANGELES, CAL.

    RECT., SMOOTH BASE, 5 ¾" and 4 ½"
    TOOLED TOP
    CLEAR
    AQUA, 5 ¾", $70.00- 2017
    COMMON

Front: THE ACME MEDICAL SUPPLY. CO. / DENVER, COLO.

    RECT., SMOOTH BASE, 5"
    TOOLED TOP
    COBALT
    RARE

Side: ADA INJECTION
Side: N & N CHEM. CO. S.F.

    RECT., SMOOTH BASE, 5 ½"
    TOOLED TOP
    AQUA
    RARE

Front: DR. H. ADOLPHUS
Side: CALIFORNIA
Re: ANTI RHEUMATIC / CORDIAL
Side: SAN FRANCISCO

    RECT., OPEN PONTIL, 7 ¼"
    APPLIED TOP
    GREENISH AQUA, $6000.00- 2008
    EX. RARE

Front: MARTHA J. ALLEN'S / FEMALE RESTORATIVE

    RECT., SMOOTH BASE, 10 ½"
    TOOLED TOP
    AQUA, $80.00- 1997
    SCARCE

Side: ALLEN'S
Front: PECTORAL / BALSAM
Side: S.F. CAL.

   RECT., SMOOTH BASE, 7"
   APPLIED TOP
   GREEN
   EX. RARE
   Note: AD FROM Jan. 1870 SAC. DAILY UNION
   NEWSPAPER. ISAAC P. ALLEN is the AGENT
   in SACRAMENTO at THIS TIME.

Side: BAILEY & EATON
Side: PARAFINE
Front: GUN OIL

   RECT., SMOOTH BASE, 3 ¾"
   APPLIED TOP
   AQUA, $120.00- 1997
   EX. RARE

Front: DR. IRA BAKER'S / COUGH BALSAM

   RECT., SMOOTH BASE, 5 ¼"
   TOOLED TOP
   AQUA
   SCARCE

Front: DR. IRA BAKER'S / FAMILY LINIMENT

   RECT., SMOOTH BASE, 5 ¼"
   TOOLED TOP
   AQUA, $20.00- 2017
   SCARCE

Front: DR. IRA BAKER'S / EMULSION COD LIVER OIL / HYPOPHOSPHATES, LIME AND SODA

    RECT., SMOOTH BASE, 8 ½"
    TOOLED TOP
    CLEAR, $80.00- 2017
    RARE

Front: S.D. BALDWIN / LINIMENT
Re: MARYSVILLE / CA.

    RECT., SMOOTH BASE, 6"
    APPLIED and TOOLED TOP
    AQUA, A.T., $700.00- 2017
    RARE with APPLIED TOP
    SCARCE with TOOLED TOP

Front: BALDWIN'S / CELERY PEPSIN / AND / DANDELION TONIC

    SQUARE, SMOOTH BASE, 8:
    TOOLED TOP
    AMBER
    COMMON
    Locale: SAN FRANCISCO
    Note: LABEL BELOW WAS TRADE MARKED in
          1897 by THE LASH'S BITTERS CO.

Front: BARKER'S CELERY KOLA
Side: PHIL BLUMAUER / PORTLAND, ORE.
Re: BARKER'S CELERY KOLA

    SQUARE, SMOOTH BASE, 10"
    TOOLED TOP
    AMBER
    SCARCE

Front: BENNET'S / MAGIC CURE

    SQUARE, SMOOTH BASE, 5"
    APPLIED TOP
    COBALT, $1500.00- 2010
    EX. RARE
    CIRCA: EARLY 1870's
    Locale: HELENA, MONT.

Front: DR. J.B. BENTON'S / LINIMENT / CARSON CITY, NEVADA

    RECT., SMOOTH BASE, 6 ½"
    TOOLED TOP
    AQUA
    EX. RARE

Front: BLISS / LIVER / AND / KIDNEY / CURE
Side: THE BLISS REMEDY CO.
Side: STOCKTON, CAL.

    RECT., SMOOTH BASE, 9 ¼"
    TOOLED TOP
    CLEAR
    EX. RARE

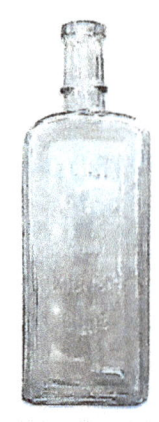
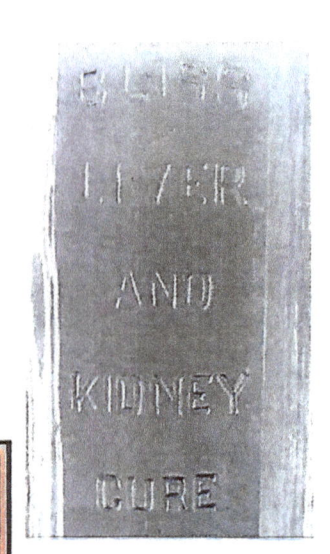

Side: BOGLE'S
Side: QUAKER BALM

    RECT., SMOOTH BASE, 6"
    TOOLED TOP
    AQUA
    SCARCE
    Note: AD FROM the 1890 S.F. DIRECTORY.

Front: BOERICKE & TAFEL'S / TRITURATIONS

    RECT., SMOOTH BASE, 7 ¾"
    APPLIED TOP
    SHADES of AMBER, AQUA
    SCARCE
    Note: THESE BOTTLES are WESTERN BLOWN.

Front: BRIGHTSBANE / THE GREAT / KIDNEY AND LIVER CURE

    RECT., SMOOTH BASE, 8 ¾"
    TOOLED TOP
    AMBER
    RARE
    Varient: "STOMACH CURE"

Front: BRO. BENJAMIN'S / HERBALO / FOR THE BLOOD / STOMACH, LIVER & KIDNEYS / RENOVATOR

    RECT., SMOOTH BAS, 8 ½"
    TOOLED TOP
    AQUA
    COMMON

Side: **DR. BOWEN'S**
Front: **BLOOD / PURIFIER**
Side: **SAN FRANCISCO**

   RECT., OPEN & IRON PONTIL, 10"
   APPLIED TOP
   GREEN
   EX. RARE
   Note: AD FROM A CIRCA 1860 NEWSPAPER, ONE OF THE FIRST WESTERN BLOWN BOTTLES.

Front: DR. BUCHARD'S / AUREOLINE / M'F'D BY JOHN ALEX
McCORMICK / SAN FRANCISCO, CAL.

    RECT., SMOOTH BASE, 6 ¾"
    TOOLED TOP
    AQUA
    COMMON

Front: BURTON'S / FAMILY / MEDICINES
Re: BURTON'S / MEDICINES

    RECT., SMOOTH BASE, 9 ½"
    TOOLED TOP
    AQUA
    SCARCE
    Locale: SACRAMENTO, CAL.

Front: BUTTE – TINE
Side: THE ABIETINE MEDICAL CO.
Side: OROVILLE, CAL. USA

    RECT., SMOOTH BASE, 6 ¼"
    AQUA
    COMMON
    CIRCA: 1894
    Note: REDINGTON & CO. WAS THE AGENT
          FOR THIS BRAND IN S.F.

Front: BURDELL'S ORIENTAL / TOOTH WASH /
        H.P. WAKELEE SOLE AGENT

    RECT., SMOOTH BASE, 6 ¾"
    APPLIED TOP
    SHADES of BLUE
    RARE
    Note: TRADE MARKED in 1869 by H.P. WAKELEE.
          THEN AGAIN in 1870 by B.B. THAYER WHO
          PUT HIS PRODUCT in a ROUND CONTAINER.

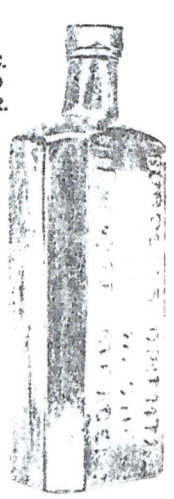

Side: BURK'S
Front: LIGHTNING / LINIMENT

    RECT., SMOOTH BASE, 7 ½"
    TOOLED TOP
    AQUA
    EX. RARE
    Locale: FRESNO, CAL.
    Note: HAS THE WESTERN CURVED R's,
    LABEL WAS TRADE MARKED in
    1879 by C.G. SAYLE of FRESNO.

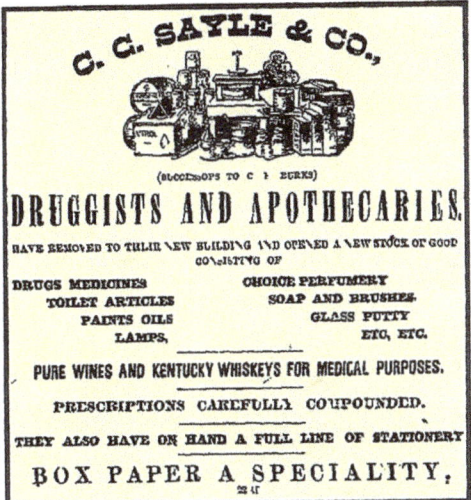

Front: NORWEGIAN COD LIVER OIL /
        IMPORTED BY / J. CALIGARIS
        PHARMACIST / S.E. COR. KEARNEY
        & PACIFIC STS. S.F.

    RECT., SMOOTH BASE, 8 ¼"
    TOOLED TOP
    CLEAR
    SCARCE

Front: COMPOUND SYRUP EUCALYPTUS /
        J. CALIGARIS / SAN FRANCISCO

    RECT., SMOOTH BASE, 7 ¾"
    TOOLED TOP
    AQUA and CLEAR
    RARE

Front: COLE'S WHITE PINE SYRUP /
        COLE & CO. / MARTINEZ, CAL.

    RECT., SMOOTH BASE, 7 ¾" and 6 ¾"
    TOOLED TOP
    AQUA, and CLEAR
    LT. AMETHYST, 6 ¾", $160.00- 2017

Side: **CAL. VOLCANIC**
Side: **MINERAL WATER CO.**

RECT., SMOOTH BASE, 6 ½"
TOOLED TOP
AQUA
RARE
Note: HAS WESTERN CURVED R's, AD FROM a 1883 PACIFIC RURAL PRESS.

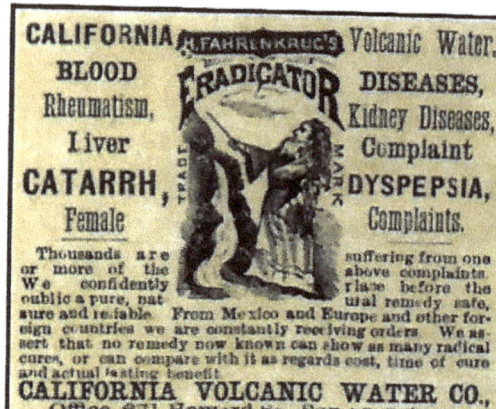

Front: **CARY / motif of TREE**
Side: **GUM TREE**
Side: **COUGH SYRUP**
Re: **SAN FRANCISCO**

RECT., SMOOTH BASE, 7"
TOOLED TOP
AQUA, $130.00- 2017
SCARCE in AQUA
RARE in LIME GREEN
Note: W.C. TYNDALE WAS the AGENT FOR THIS BRAND in SAN FRANCISCO. LABEL AT RIGHT TRADE MARKED in 1883. TYNDALE ALSO TRADE MARKED THIS LABEL FOR MOTHER CARY'S SALVE IN 1882.

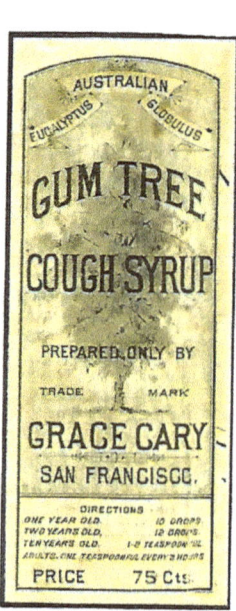
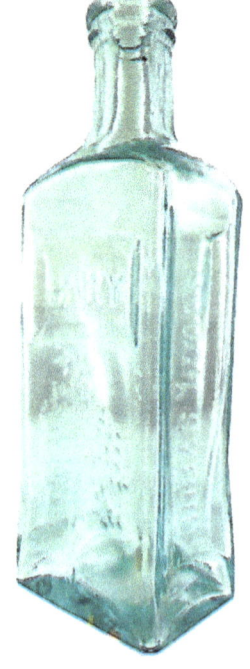

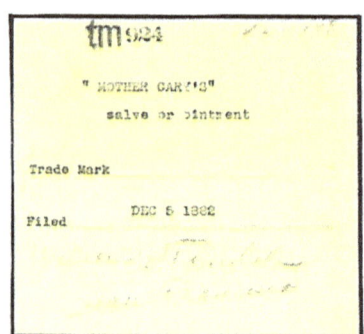

Front: C.C. LINIMENT / THE W.H. BONE CO. /
SAN FRANCISCO, CAL.

ROUND, SMOOTH BASE, 5 ½"
TOOLED TOP
SCARCE in AQUA, $50.00- 2002
RARE in GREEN and AMBER
Note: LABEL TRADE MARKED IN 1888.
   AD. IS FROM THE JULY 12, 1890 SONOMA
   DEMOCRAT NEWSPAPER.

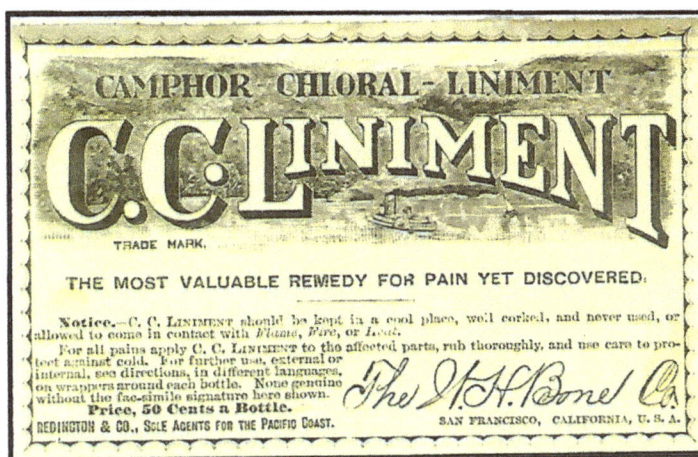

Front: CELRO – KOLA CO. / PORTLAND, ORE.
Side: CELRO – KOLA (in script)
Side: CELRO – KOLA (in script)

SQUARE, SMOOTH BASE, 10"
TOOLED TOP
AMBER
SCARCE

Front: DR. E. CHAMPLAIN'S / LIGNEOUS
   EXTRACT / PATENTED

OVAL, SMOOTH BASE, 5 ¼"
APPLIED TOP
DEEP AQUA, $250.00- 2017
SCARCE
Locale: CLOVERDALE, CAL., HAS THE
   WESTERN CURVED R's

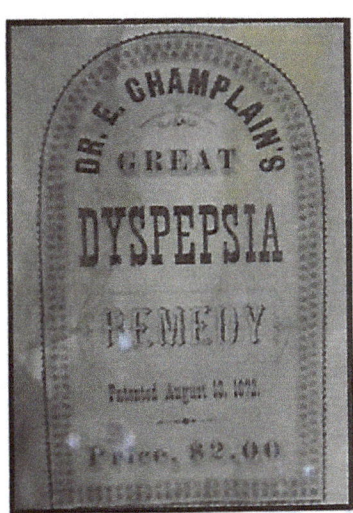
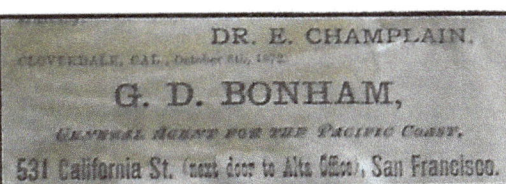

Front: **CLOVER LEAF / CATARRH REMEDY**

    RECT., SMOOTH BASE, 3 ½"
    TOOLED TOP
    CLEAR
    RARE
    Locale: CLOVERDALE, CAL.

Side: **WM. A. CLARK'S**
Front: **INTERNAL / AND / EXTERNAL**
Side: **S.F. = CAL.**
Re: motif of SNAKE

    RECT., SMOOTH BASE, 6 ½"
    APPLIED TOP
    AQUA
    EX. RARE
    Note: HAS THE WESTERN CURVED R's

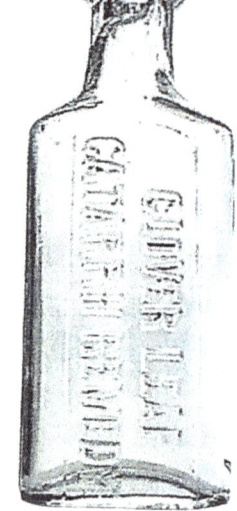

Side: **WM. A. CLARK**
Front: **HORSE LINIMENT**
Side: **S.F. CAL.**
Re: **FOR MAN OR BEAST**

    RECT., SMOOTH BASE, 7"
    APPLIED TOP
    AQUA
    EX. RARE

Front: **CONNELL'S / BRAHMINICAL / MOONPLANT / EAST INDIAN / REMEDIES**
Re: "motif of STARS around TWO FEET" / TRADE MARK

    OVAL, SMOOTH BASE, 8 ½"
    APPLIED TOP
    AMBER, $550.00- 2003
          $1100.00- 2011 (with label)
    RARE
    Note: HAS THE WESTERN CURVED R's

Front: JOHN W. COPE'S / MT. SHASTA KIDNEY / AND LIVER CURE

RECT., SMOOTH BASE, 8 ½"
TOOLED TOP
AQUA
EX. RARE
Locale: STOCKTON, CAL.

Front: THE JOHN W. COPE CO. / STOCKTON, CAL.
Re: BEST IN THE WORLD

SQUARE, SMOOTH BASE, 9 ½"
TOOLED TOP
AMBER, $180.00- 2007
RARE
Note: ALL ADS CIRCA 1896.

Front: CROCKETT'S / AMYGDALINE
Side: J.R. GATES & CO.
Side: PROPRIETORS

RECT., SMOOTH BASE, 7"
APPLIED and TOOLED TOP
AQUA, TOOLED TOP, $300.00- 2017
RARE
Locale: SACRAMENTO, CAL.

Front: CROCKETT'S / AMYGDALINE
Side: R. HALL & CO.
Side: PROPRIETORS

RECT., SMOOTH BASE, 7" and 4 ½"
APPLIED TOP
AQUA, 7", $200.00- 2003
RARE in the 7" SIZE
EX. RARE in the SMALL SIZE

Side: COWAN & FLINT'S
Side: AGUE KING

RECT., SMOOTH BASE, 8 ¼"
APPLIED TOP
AQUA
EX. RARE
Locale: MARYSVILLE, CAL.
Note: AD FROM 1867 DIRECTORY
NEWSPAPER AD FROM THE JUNE
22, 1873 MARYSVILLE DAILY APPEAL.

Front: DR. / CURLISS (in indented panel)
Side: RHEUMATIC REMEDY
Side: SAN FRANCISCO

RECT., SMOOTH BASE, 7"
APPLIED TOP
AQUA
EX. RARE

Front: CURTIS / COUGH / CURE
Side: C.C.C.
Side: C.C.C.
Re: J.J. MACK & CO. / SOLE
  PROPRIETORS / SAN
  FRANCISCO, CAL.

RECT., SMOOTH BASE, 6"
TOOLED TOP
AQUA, $110.00- 1997
SCARCE

Side: D.D.D.

RECT., SMOOTH BASE, 7 ¼"
TOOLED TOP
RARE in COBALT, $100.00- 2010
SCARCE in AQUA
Note: THIS BOTTLE WAS DUG IN THE SAN
  JOSE, CAL. AREA AND APPEARS TO BE
  WESTERN BLOWN.

Front: **DRS. DARRIN / ELECTRO – MAGNETIC / PHYSICIANS / PORTLAND, OR. & SEATTLE, W.T.**

    RECT., SMOOTH BASE, 6 ¾"
    TOOLED TOP
    CLEAR
    EX. RARE
    CIRCA: 1886-1888

Front: **ONE OF THE DEBECO / REMEDIES**

    RECT., SMOOTH BASE, 5 ¼"
    TOOLED TOP
    AMBER
    SCARCE
    Locale: DENVER, COLO.

Front: **J.D. EASTMAN & CO. / DEER LODGE, MONTANA**

    SQUARE, SMOOTH BASE, 8 ¾"
    APPLIED TOP
    AMBER, $1000.00- 2003
    EX. RARE

Front: **DOCTOR ELLIS**

    ROUND, SMOOTH BASE, 6"
    FLAIRED TOP
    AQUA
    EX. RARE
    Note: REPORTEDLY FROM ANAHEIM, CAL., BOTTLE IS BELIEVED TO BE ENGLISH BLOWN.

Front: **ELY'S / WILD CHERRY / PHOSPHATE**
Side: **W.T. ELY & CO.**
Side: **SAN FRANCISCO**

    RECT., SMOOTH BASE, 6 ¼"
    TOOLED TOP
    AQUA
    LT. LIME GREEN, $80.00- 1996
    RARE

Front: **FAIR'S / PNEUMONIA / MIXTURE**

    RECT., SMOOTH BASE, 5 ¾"
    TOOLED TOP
    CLEAR
    RARE
    Locale: BUTTE, MONTANA

Front: **FARQUAR'S / MEDICATED**
Side: **WINE & BRANDY**
Side: **CALIFORNIA**

    SQUARE, SMOOTH BASE, 9 ¼"
    APPLIED TOP
    REDDISH PUCE, $2100.00- 1995
                          $1600.00- 1996
    EX. RARE

Side: FARMER'S
Front: HORSE MEDICINE / S.F. CAL
Side: XXX

RECT., SMOOTH BASE, 8 ¼" and 6 ¾"
TOOLED and APPLIED TOP
LT. GREEN, T.T., 6 ¾", $130.00- 2017
AQUA, 6 ¾", A.T., $110.00- 2017
AQUA, 8 ¼", T.T., $30.00- 2017
COMMON with a TOOLED TOP
SCARCE with an APPLIED TOP
Note: TRADE CARDS BELOW and at NEAR RIGHT. AD LOWER RIGHT SHOWING PRODUCTS THAT HOMER WILLIAM SWAS AN AGENT FOR IN 1875. THIS INCLUDED FARMER'S HORSE MEDICINE. THIS AD ID FROM THE MARIPOSA GAZETTE, JUNE 12, 1875.

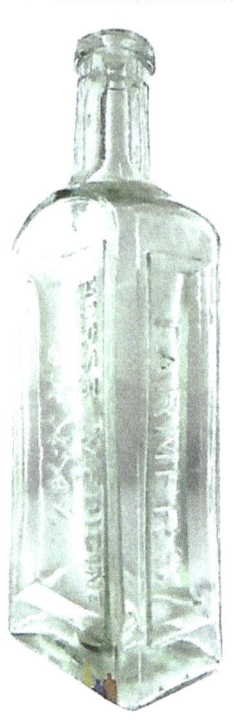

Front: 95 – F.F.F. / BALM OF MECCA / EMBROCATION / 1889

RECT., SMOOTH BASE, 6 ¼"
TOOLED TOP
AQUA
RARE

Front: FARMER'S HEALING LINIMENT / GRAHAM & FISH / LODI, CALIFORNIA

RECT., SMOOTH BASE, 8 ¾"
TOOLED TOP
AQUA, $160.00- 2017
SCARCE
Note: LABEL DRAWING WAS TRADE MARKED in 1888 BY GRAHAM & FISH, LODI CAL.

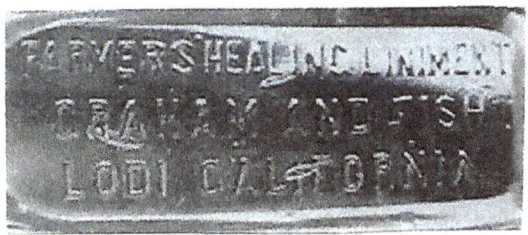

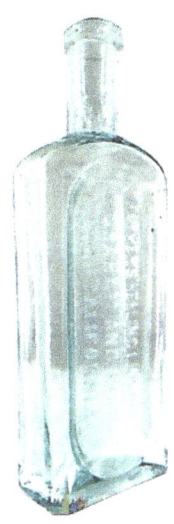

Front: motif of hand / F. & CO.
Side: HELPING
Side: HAND

RECT., SMOOTH BASE, 5 ½"
APPLIED TOP
AQUA
EX. RARE
Note: IF THIS BOTTLE HAD an R it WOULD NO DOUBT BE CURVED, AS IT HAS THE SAME FAT FLAT LETTERING STYLE AS OTHER WESTERN BLOW BOTTLES HAVE. IT WAS TRADE MARKED IN 1873 BY WILLIAM FRISBIE IN SANTA CLARA CAL. LETTER WITH THE T/M APPLICATION STATES THE IMAGE OF A HAND WITH THE PALM OUT WILL BE PRESENT. F & CO. ON THE BOTTLE HAS TO BE MR. FRISBIE.

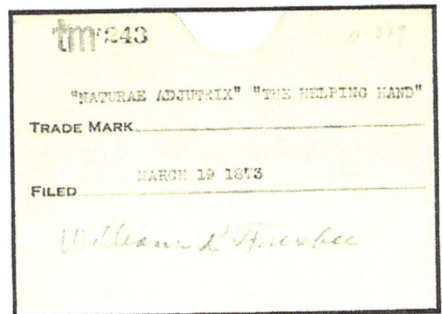

Front: DR. A.E. FLINT'S / HEART REMEDY /
J.J. MACK & CO. PROP'S / SAN
FRANCISCO

RECT., SMOOTH BASE, 7 ½"
TOOLED TOP
AMBER, $90.00- 2017
SCARCE

Front: FORCE'S ASTH – MANNA / TRADE MARK REG. /
ASTHMA, BRONCHITIS, COLDS, ETC. /
S.B. FORCE M'F'G CHEMIST /
SAN FRANCISCO, CAL.

SQUARE, SMOOTH BASE, 8 ¾"
TOOLED TOP
AMBER, $130.00- 2005
Note: THERE ARE 3 VARIENTS OF THIS BOTTLE.
ALL ARE COMMON. LABEL TRADE
MARKED in 1898 by S.B. FORCE S.F.

Front: FRY'S FAMILY MEDICINES /
SALEM, OREGON

RECT., SMOOTH BASE, 7"
TOOLED TOP
AQUA, $90.00- 2006
RARE

Front: FRY'S LIGHTNING HEALER /
SALEM, OREGON

RECT., SMOOTH BASE, 7"
TOOLED TOP
AQUA
RARE

Side: DR. AH FUNG'S
Front: GREAT / CHINESE REMEDY
Side: J.S. McCUE AGENTS S.F.

RECT., SMOOTH BASE, 6"
APPLIED TOP
AQUA
EX. RARE
Note: HAS THE WESTERN CURVED R's

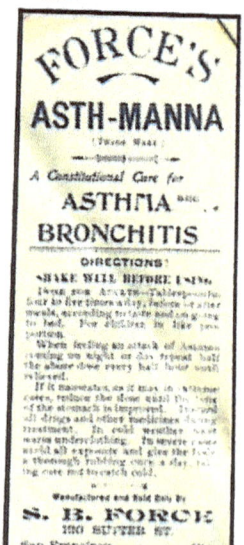
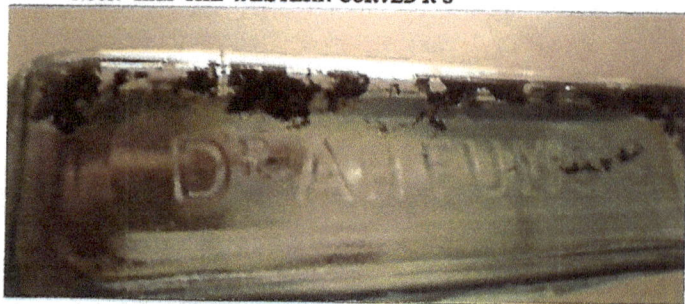

Side: **DR. FURBUR'S**
Front: **CORDIAL OF / MOUNTAIN BALM**
Side: **YREKA**

RECT., SMOOTH BASE, 8"
APPLIED TOP
AQUA, $700.00- 1997 (potstone)
EX. RARE
Note: AD is CIRCA 1870. DR. FURBER ALSO HAD AN OFFICE in VALLEJO, CAL in the EARLY 1870's. I KNOW of 2 WHOLE SPECIMENS BEING DUG THERE in the 1970's. THIS BRAND WAS ALSO DISTRIBUTED IN S.F.

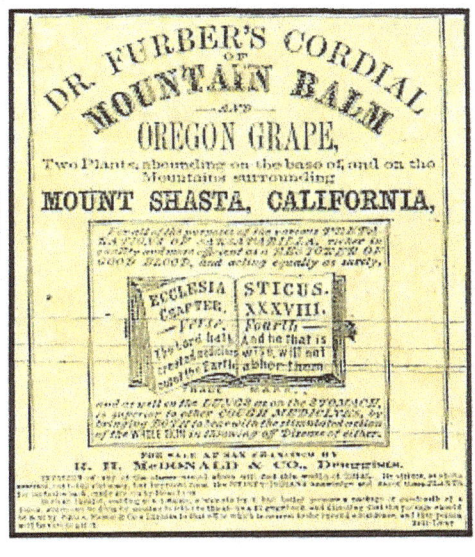

Front: **FULTON'S / RADICAL REMEDY**
Re: **SURE KIDNEY, LIVER / AND DYSPEPSIA CURE**

SQUARE, SMOOTH BASE, 9"
APPLIED TOP
AMBER
EX. RARE
Locale: SAN FRANCISCO

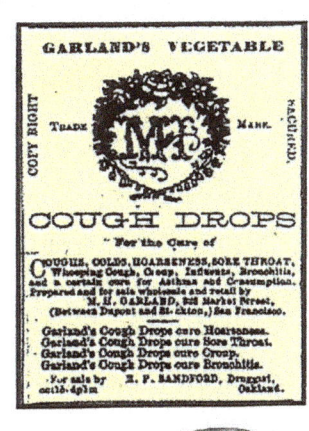

Front: **GARLAND'S / COUGH DROPS**

RECT., SMOOTH BASE, 7 ¼"
APPLIED TOP
AQUA, $400.00- 2006
 D.C.T., $180.00- 2017
RARE
Note: AD is CIRCA 1868

Front: **GOGINGS / monogram / IRON / TONIC / 904 J ST. / SACRAMENTO**

RECT., SMOOTH BASE, 8"
TOOLED TOP
AQUA, $70.00- 1997
SCARCE
Locale: SACRAMENTO, CAL
Note: LABEL TRADE MARKED IN 1890.

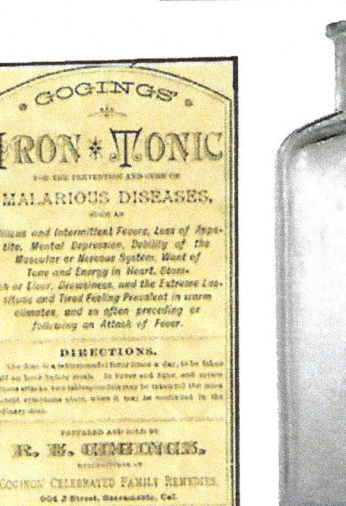

Front: GOGING'S / WILD CHERRY TONIC

    SQUARE, SMOOTH BASE, 8 ¾"
    TOOLED TOP
    AMBER
    SCARCE
    Locale: SACRAMENTO, CAL.

Front: GOLDEN GATE MEDICAL SYRUP
Side: B.F. ROBERTS & CO.
Side: CALIFORNIA

    RECT., SMOOTH BASE, 10"
    TOOLED TOP
    AQUA, $60.00- 2017
    SCARCE
    Note: THIS BRAND WAS TRADE MARKED in
    1889 BY B.F. ROBERTS of SANTA ROSA, CAL.

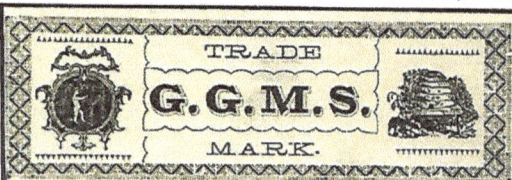

Base: DR. GRATTAN

    ROUND, SMOOTH BASE, 8 ¾"
    APPLIED TOP
    DEEP OLIVE AMBER, $600.00- 2008
    Locale: STOCKTON, CAL., and has the
    WESTERN CURVED R's

Side: DR. C. GRATTAN'S
Front: DIPTHERIA
Side: REMEDY

    RECT., SMOOTH BASE, 6 ¾"
    APPLIED and TOOLED TOP
    AQUA, APPLIED TOP, $425.00- 2010
    AQUA, TOOLED TOP, $70.00- 2017
    SCARCE
    Locale: STOCKTON, CAL., LABEL was
    TRADE MARKED in 1867.

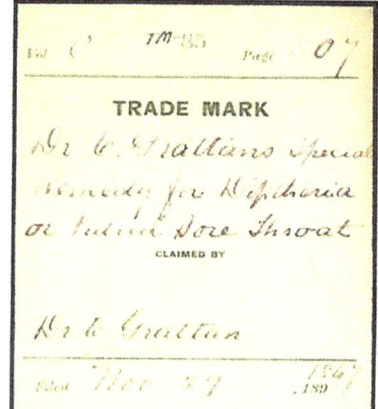

Side: GUPTILL'S
Side: SURE CURE

    RECT., SMOOTH BASE, 4 ½"
    APPLIED TOP
    AQUA
    EX. RARE
    LOCALE: SAN FRANCISCO

Front: **GREEN'S LUNG RESTORER / SANTA ABIE**
Side: **ABIETINE MEDICAL CO.**
Side: **OROVILLE, CAL. USA**

    RECT., SMOOTH BASE, 8" and 6 ¼"
    TOOLED TOP
    LT. GREEN, 8", $1200.00- 2017
    AQUA, 6 ¼", $70.00- 2017
    SCARCE in AQUA
    RARE in GREENS
    Note: LABEL AT RIGHT WAS TRADE
      MARKED IN 1884. EARLY TRADE
      IN THE MIDDLE. AD AT BOTTOM
      RIGHT CIRCA 1889.

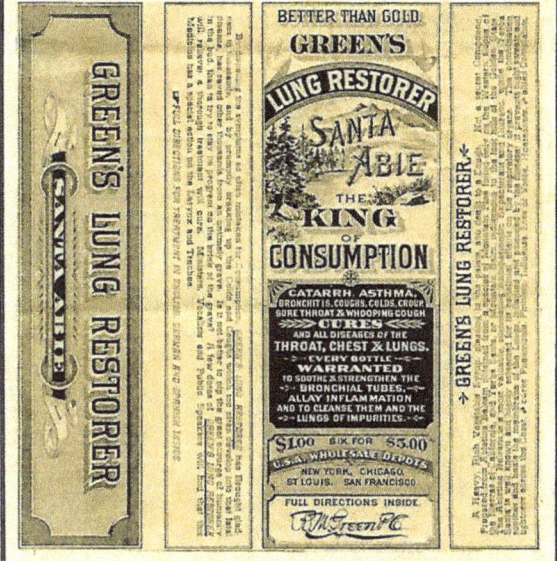
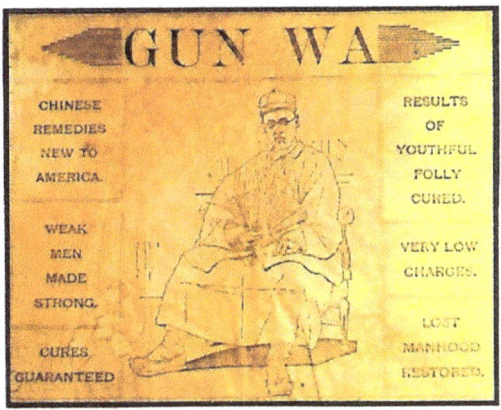

Front: **GUN WA'S / CHINESE REMEDY**
Re: **WARRENTED / ENTIRELY
    VEGTABLE / AND HARMLESS**

    SQUARE., SMOOTH BASE, 9 ¾" and 8 ¼"
    APPLIED TOP
    YELLOW AMBER, 9 ¾", $1600.00- 2015
    YELLOW AMBER, 8 ¾", $1100.00- 2019
    LT. YELLOW GREEN, 8 ¼", 1300.00- 2017
    SCARCE in the SMALL SIZE
    RARE in the LARGE SIZE
    Locale: DENVER, COLO.
    Note: AD is CIRCA 1889, THESE BOTTLES
      WERE REPORTEDLY BLOWN at THE
      COLORADO GLASS WORKS in GOLDEN.

Front: **GUN WA'S / CHINESE / HERB / & /
    VEGETABLE / REMEDIES**

    SQUARE, SMOOTH BASE, 6 ½"
    TOOLED TOP
    AMBER
    RARE
    Locale: DENVER, COLO.

Front: G.W.H. (on shoulder)

    ROUND, SMOOTH BASE, 8"
    APPLIED TOP
    COBALT
    RARE
    Note: DUG in SAN LUIS OBISPO and the LETTERS
    HAVE A WESTERN STYLE FONT.

Front: HALL'S / PULMONARY / BALSAM
Side: J.R. GATES & CO.
Side: PROPRIETORS S.F.

    RECT., SMOOTH BASE, 6 ¼"
    APPLIED and TOOLED TOP
    AQUA, APPLIED TOP, $60.00- 2017
    AQUA, TOOLED TOP, $30.00- 2019
    COMMON
    Note: HAS THE WESTERN CURVED R's
    Varient: SHEPARDSON & GATES ARE
        THE AGENTS, THESE ARE SCARCE

Front: HALL'S / HEPATIC KING
Side: J.R. GATES & CO.
Side: PROPRIETORS

    RECT., SMOOTH BASE, 6 ½"
    TOOLED TOP
    AQUA, $325.00- 2019
    RARE

Front: VALENTINE HASSMER'S / LUNG
    & COUGH SYRUP / PRICE PER
    BOTTLE $1.25 / 5 BOTTLES TO
    A GALLON / P.O. BOX 1886

    ROUND, SMOOTH BASE, 11"
    APPLIED AND TOOLED TOP
    AMBER, $325.00- 2017
    Note: LABEL TRADE MARKED in 1881
    Note: APPLIED TOP EXAMPLES HAVE THE
        WESTERN CURVED R's

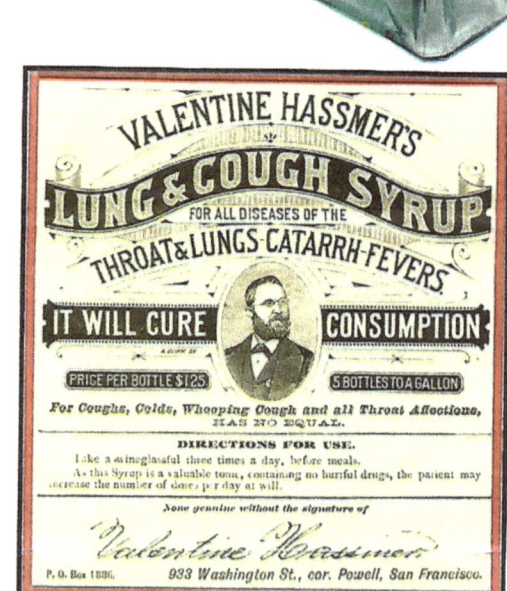

Front: HASWELL'S / WITCH HAZEL
    CREAM

    RECT., SMOOTH BASE, 6"
    TOOLED TOP
    AQUA
    SCARCE
    Locale: DENVER, COLO.

Front: LEON HAVE'S / STRATENA

    ROUND, SMOOTH BASE, 2 ½"
    APPLIED TOP
    AQUA
    RARE
    Note: HAS THE WESTERN CURVED R's

Front: B.R. HATHAWAY & CO. / PROP'RS / SAN FRANCISCO, CAL.
Side: DR. SWEET'S
Side: LIVER CLEANSER

   RECT., SMOOTH BASE, 8"
   TOOLED TOP
   AQUA
   EX. RARE
   Note: HAS THE WESTERN CURVED R's
   Note: THE LABEL AT RIGHT WAS TRADE MARKED IN 1900
         ACCORDING TO THE ACOMPANING LETTER, IT HAS
         BEEN IN USE SINCE 1872. IT MENTIONS TWO
         REMEDIES OF WHICH THE LIVER CLEANSER MAY
         BE THE OTHER.

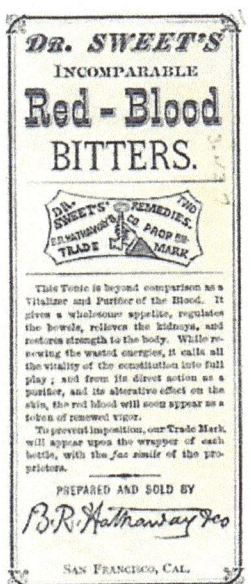

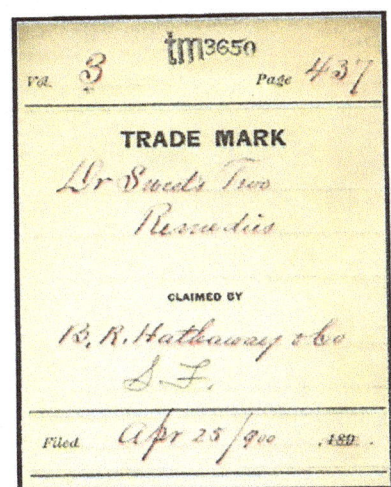

Front: HICKORY BARK / COUGH REMEDY
Side: SALEM, ORE. USA
Side: NO NARCOTICS / ALCOHOL

   RECT., SMOOTH BASE, 5 ¾"
   TOOLED TOP
   AQUA
   RARE

Front: HEPATIC KING
Side: J.R. GATES & CO.
Side: PROPRIETORS

    RECT., SMOOTH BASE, 6 ½"
    APPLIED TOP
    AQUA
    EX. RARE
    Note: HAS THE WESTERN CURVED R's

Side: HERBS OF LIFE
Side: BLOOD PURIFIER / DENVER, COLO. USA

    RECT., SMOOTH BASE, 8 ¾"
    APPLIED TOP
    AQUA
    SCARCE

Front: DR. HENRY'S BOTANIC / PREPARATIONS

    RECT., SMOOTH BASE, 6 ¼"
    APPLIED TOP
    AQUA, $500.00- 2017
    RARE

Front: DR. HILLER'S / COUGH CURE

    RECT., SMOOTH BASE, 7 ¼"
    TOOLED TOP
    AQUA
    RARE
    CIRCA: 1886

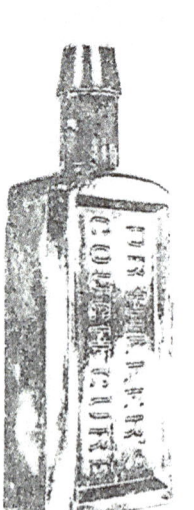

Front: DR. HILLER'S / HYDRASTINE / RESTORATIVE

    RECT., SMOOTH BASE, 8"
    TOOLED TOP
    AMBER
    EX. RARE
    CIRCA: 1884

Side: DOCTOR HENLEY'S
Side: DANDELION TONIC

    RECT., SMOOTH BASE, 9"
    TOOLED TOP
    AMBER, $200.00- 2009
    SCARCE

Side: DR. HENLEY'S / CELERY,
       BEEF AND IRON
Side: C.B. & I. EXTRACT CO. / S.F. CAL.

    RECT., SMOOTH BASE, 9 ½"
    APPLIED and TOOLED TOP
    AMBER, T.T., $150.00- 2005
    AMBER, A.T., $800.00- 2015
    SCARCE
    Note: LABEL TRADE MARKED in 1885

Front: DR. HENLEY'S / CELERY,
        BEEF & IRON

    ROUND, SMOOTH BASE, 11 ¾"
    APPLIED and TOOLED TOP
    AMBER, A.T., $40.00- 2003
    SCARCE
    Note: EARLY TRADE CARD AT UPPER
          RIGHT, LABEL WAS TRADE
          MARKED in 1883.

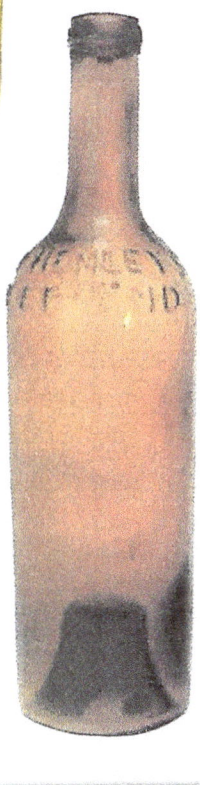

Front: **DR. HENLEY'S / REGULATOR**

SQUARE, SMOOTH BASE, 8 ½"
APPLIED TOP
AQUA
EX. RARE
Note: AD at RIGHT is CIRCA 1867.

BELOW IS AN AD FOR DR. HENLEY'S TAMARACK. NO EMBOSSED BOTTLES FOR THIS PRODUCT HAVE SURFACED TO DATE. IT MAY HAVE BEEN A LABEL ONLY ITEM, BUT WHO KNOWS? THAT ELUSIVE SUPER RARE HENLEY BOTTLE MAY STILL BE OUT THERE FOR SOME LUCKY DIGGER.

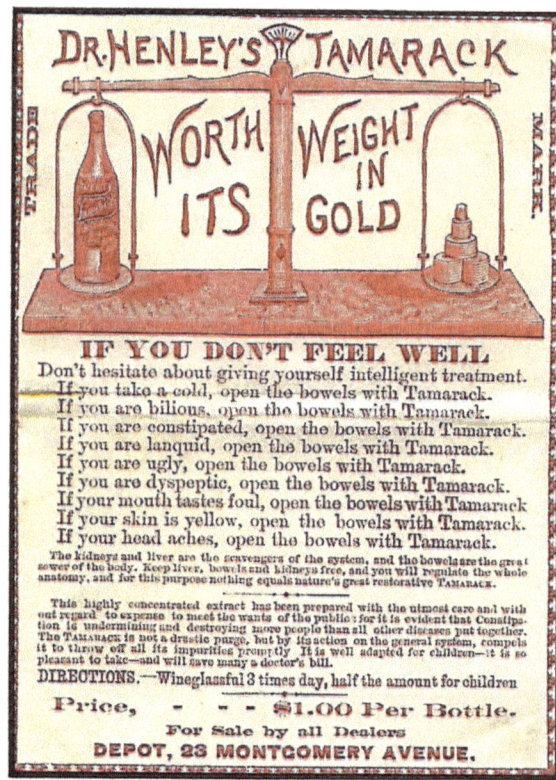

Side: **HENLEY'S**
Front: **ROYAL**
Side: **BALSAM**

RECT., SMOOTH BASE, 7"
APPLIED TOP
AQUA, $475.00 - 2003
EX. RARE
Note: LABEL at RIGHT TRADE MARKED in 1867, SAME AS THE DATE FOR AD SHOWN.

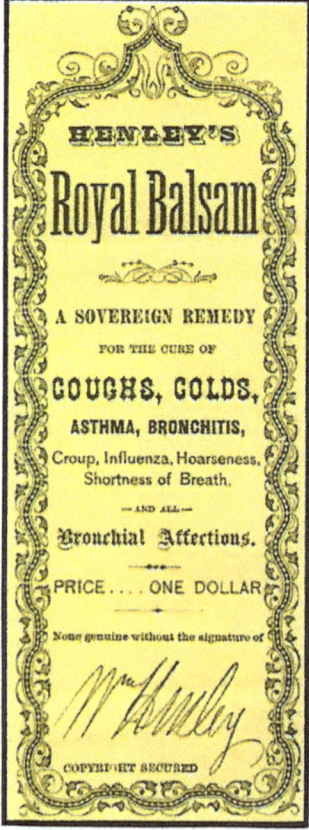

Front: **HILMER'S / POPULAR REMEDY / SAN FRANCISCO**

    RECT., SMOOTH BASE, 7 ¼"
    TOOLED TOP
    AQUA
    RARE
    CIRCA: 1884

Front: **HILMER'S LABORATORY / SAN FRANCISCO**
    (on shoulder)

    ROUND, SMOOTH BASE, 8 ½"
    APPLIED and TOOLED TOP
    AQUA
    RARE

Front: **HOLDEN'S / ETHEREAL COUGH SYRUP**
Side: **THE HOLDEN DRUG CO.**
Side: **STOCKTON, CAL.**

    RECT., SMOOTH BASE, 6"
    TOOLED TOP
    AQUA
    SCARCE

HOLDEN'S ETHEREAL COUGH SYRUP

For all throat and lung affections. Pleasant to take; quick relief. For more than 60 years the standard cough remedy of San Joaquin Valley.

THREE SIZES
25c, 50c, $1.00

Money Back if not pleased with results

THE HOLDEN DRUG STORES
PHONE 1
Main and El Dorado Sts.
Elks' Building   Stockton, Cal.

Front: **HOLDEN'S / DYSENTARY / & DIARRHOEA / CORDIAL**

    ROUND, OPEN PONTIL, 5"
    APPLIED TOP
    AQUA
    EX. RARE
    Locale: STOCKTON, CAL.

Side: **HOP – CEL COMPANY / SAN FRANCISCO**
Side: **NERVE, BLOOD & BRAIN TONIC**

    RECT., SMOOTH BASE, 9" and 10 ¾"
    TOOLED TOP
    AMBER, 10 ¾", $100.00- 2017
    SCARCE

Front: **DR. JEROME HORN / MAGNETIC / HEALING BATHS / 808 24th ST. / NEAR MISSION / SAN FRANCISCO**

    OVAL, SMOOTH BASE, 4"
    TOOLED TOP
    CLEAR
    RARE

Front: THE / CELEBRATED
Side: D.D.T. 1868
Side: HORSE MEDICINE
Re: H.H.H.

    RECT., SMOOTH BASE, 6 ¾" and 8 ¼"
    APPLIED and TOOLED TOP
    SHADES of AQUA and GREEN
    AQUA, A.T., 6 ¾", $110.00- 2017
    TOOLED TOPS are COMMON
    APPLIED TOPS are SCARCE
    Varient: MISSPELLED 'MEDICINE'
    Note: HAS the WESTERN CURVED R's,
    FIRST TRADE MARKED In 1868 BY
    DANIEL DODGE TOMLINSON of
    STOCKTON. SEE AD at RIGHT.
    LABEL was TRADE MARKED In 1880
    BY HENRY MOORE of STOCKTON.
    LABEL at LOWER RIGHT

Front: THE CELEBRATED / H.H.H.
    HORSE / MEDICINE /
    D,D.T. 1868

    RECT., SMOOTH BASE, 8 ¼"
    TOOLED TOP
    BLUE and AQUA
    RARE
    Note: THIS VARIENT WAS DISTRIBUTED
    IN THE MIDWEST, BUT THEY
    HAVE ALSO BEEN DUG IN
    CALIFORNIA.

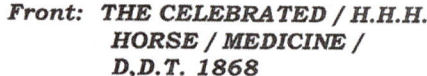

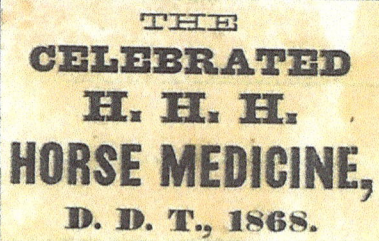

Front: H.H.H. HORSE / MEDICINE
Side: D.D.T. 1868

    RECT., SMOOTH BASE, 5 ¾" and 6 ¼"
    TOOLED TOP
    LIME GREEN, 6 ¼", $275.00- 2010
    AQUA, 6 ¼", $60.00- 2017
    COMMON in the LARGER SIZE
    SCARCE in the SMALLER SIZE

Front: H.H.H. / HORSE MEDICINE
Side: THE CELEBRATED
Side: D.D.T. 1868

    RECT., SMOOTH BASE, 9 ¼"
    APPLIED TOP
    DEEP AQUA, $1100.00- 2017 (chip)
    EX. RARE in the LARGE SIZE

Front: IMPERIAL EMBROCATION / FOR VETERINARY USE / THE ACME MEDICAL SUPPLY CO. / DENVER, COLO.

    RECT., SMOOTH BASE, 5 ½"
    TOOLED TOP
    COBALT
    RARE

Front: INDAIN WIGWAM REMEDIES / SNAKE ROOT OIL LINIMENT / M.S.M. & I. CO. / DENVER, COLORADO

    ROUND, SMOOTH BASE, 5 ½"
    TOOLED TOP
    AQUA
    RARE

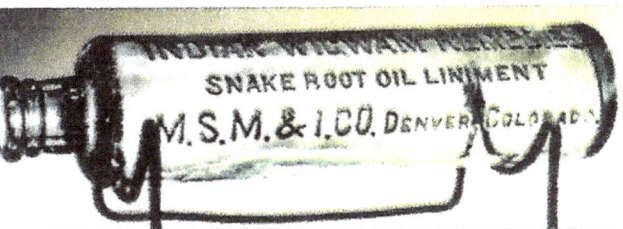

Front: INDAIN WIGWAM REMEDIES / COMPOUNDED
Re: MINERAL SPRING M. & I. CO. / DENVER, COLO.

    SQUARE, SMOOTH BASE, 8"
    APPLIED TOP
    AMBER, $850.00- 2017
    EX. RARE

Side: INDIAN COUGH SYRUP
Side: WARM SPRINGS, OREGON

    RECT., SMOOTH BASE, 6 ¾"
    TOOLED TOP
    AQUA, $50.00- 1996
    RARE
    Note: NO PIC AVAILABLE

Side: **JAFFE'S ELECTRIC**
Side: **PAIN EXPELLER**

    RECT., SMOOTH BASE, 7 ¼" and 5 ¼"
    TOOLED TOP
    AQUA
    SCARCE in BOTH SIZES
    Note: LABEL TRADE MARKED in 1892 by
         M.S. JAFFE of SAN JOSE. JAFFE
         HAD ANOTHER PRODUCT TRADE
         MARKED in 1893. JAFFE'S
         ELECTRIC TONIC. SEE PIC BELOW.
         THEY PROBABLY WERE PUT UP IN
         THE SAME BOTTLE.

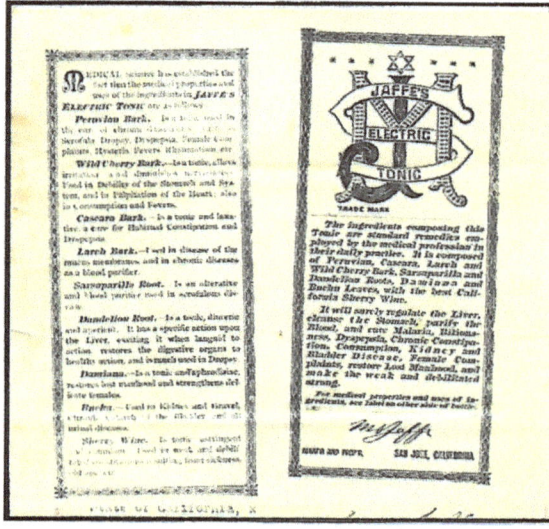
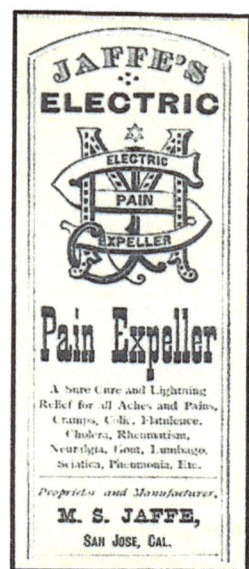

Front: **JAPANESE REMEDY**
Re: THE MIKADO TONIC

    SQUARE, SMOOTH BASE, 8 ¾"
    APPLIED TOP
    AMBER, $120.00 - 1995
    RARE

Front: **W.M. JOHNSON'S / PURE HERB TONIC /
        SURE CURE / FOR ALL MALARIAL
        DISEASES**

    SQUARE, SMOOTH BASE, 8 ½"
    TOOLED TOP
    AMBER, $110.00 - 1995
    SCARCE

Front: **JOY'S EMULSION / COD LIVER OIL WITH /
HYPOPHOSPHITES**
Side: **EDWIN W. JOY**
Side: **CHEMIST, S.F.**

RECT., SMOOTH BASE, 9"
TOOLED TOP
AQUA, $275.00- 1992
RARE
Note: EDWIN JOY TRADE MARKED THIS LABEL
FOR HIS COUGH CURE in 1888. NO
BOTTLE HAS COME TO LIGHT AS OF
NOW. HE WAS ALSO AN AGENT FOR
OTHER PRODUCTS AS THE TRADE CARD
SHOWS. CIRCA 1890's.

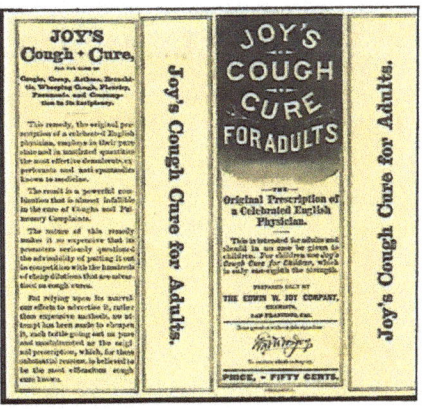

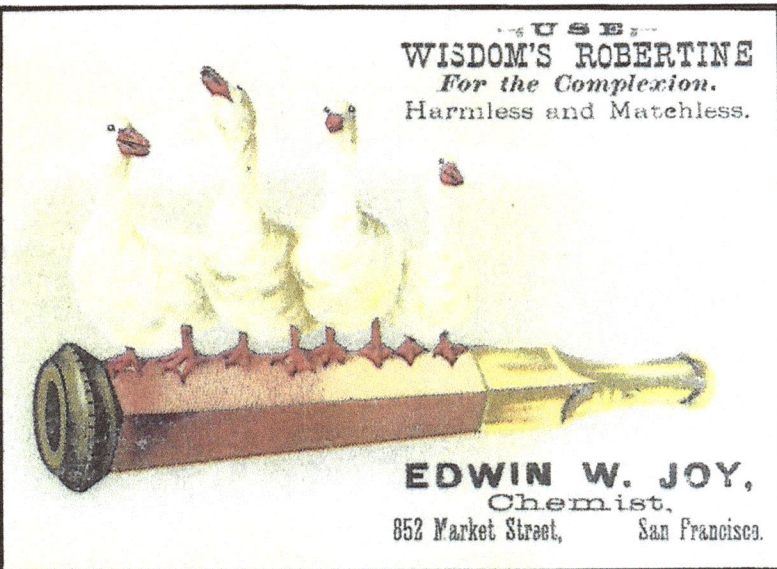

Front: **DR. KELLY'S / MEDICINES**

OVAL, OPEN PONTIL, 7 ½"
APPLIED TOP
AQUA, $550.00- 2017
EX. RARE

Front: **KETCHAM'S / COUGH SYRUP /
CLOSSON & KELLY /
SEATTLE, WASH.**

RECT., SMOOTH BASE, 6 ½"
TOOLED TOP
AQUA
RARE
CIRCA: 1892 - 1895

Front: **KRONBERGER'S / GREEN LIQUID /
FOR CORNS**

SQUARE, SMOOTH BASE, 2 ¼"
TOOLED TOP
CLEAR
SCARCE
Locale: SAN RAFAEL, CAL.

Side: **DR. KAISER'S**
Front: **GERMAN ELIXIR**
Side: **TOLEDO O.**

RECT., SMOOTH BASE, 6 ½"
APPLIED TOP
AQUA, $600.00- 2017
RARE in AQUA
EX. RARE in LIME GREEN
Note: HAS THE WESTERN CURVED R's.
EARLY TRADE CARD TAKES AWAY
ANY DOUBT ABOUT THIS BEING A
SAN FRANCISCO BOTTLE.

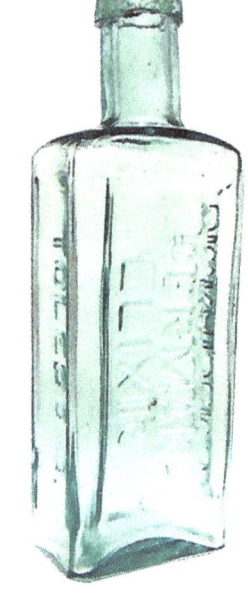

THEY ALL TAKE IT.

When the system is run down to that extent that you pass sleepless nights, are nervous and irritable, have gloomy forebodings, sour stomach, sick headache and coated tongue, do not enroll yourself as high private, in the rear rank, under General Debility, but cheer up and try

WHITE'S PRAIRIE FLOWER,

The Great Liver Panacea, now for sale in every city and town on the Continent. No medicine ever compounded is half its equal for the cure of

DYSPEPSIA & LIVER COMPLAINT

It has a specific power over the liver, and by curing the Liver, Dyspepsia and all other diseases arising from it, vanish as if by magic.
Sample bottles are sold at the small price of 25 cents that will convince you of its merit. Large size bottles 75 cents, for sale everywhere.

THE GREAT GERMAN REMEDY!
THE CELEBRATED
GERMAN ELIXIR

but recently introduced on the American Continent, has no equal in the world for the cure of

Throat and Lung Diseases, Consumption, Bronchitis, Bleeding of the Lungs; Coughs, Colds, &c.

A single trial will convince you of its great merit. It is rich in the medicinal properties of Tar, Wild Cherry, etc.
This valuable medicine is now sold in every City and Town on the Continent, at the low price of 25 cents for trial size. Large size bottles 75c. The directions are in full around each bottle. Be sure you get only German Elixir. The genuine bears the Prussian Coat of Arms, the fac-simile signature of DR. AUG. KAISER, and has his name blown on every 75c. bottle.

CHANNING WHITE,
PROPRIETOR.
TOLEDO, OHIO, and SAN FRANCISCO, CAL.

Front: **LAGENBACH'S / DYSENTARY CURE**
(embossed vertically)

ROUND, SMOOTH BASE, 4 ½"
TOOLED TOP
AMBER
SCARCE
Locale: SAN FRANCISCO

Side: DR. LAMEROUX'S
Side: PALMETTO OIL
Front: CRANE & BRIGHAM / WHOLESALE
DRUGGISTS / SAN FRANCISCO

RECT., SMOOTH BASE, 6 ¾" and 5 ¼"
APPLIED TOP
AQUA, 6 ¾", $375.00- 2009
AQUA, 5 ¼", $275.00- 2017
RARE in BOTH SIZES

Side: DR. LECHNER'S
Side: ARCANUM

RECT., SMOOTH BASE, 6 ¼"
APPLIED TOP (I'm guessing here)
AQUA
EX. RARE
Note: HAS the WESTERN CURVED R's.
THE LABEL BELOW WAS TRADE
MARKED in 1884 by the ARCANUM
MEDICINE CO. S.F.

Side: DR. LEPPER'S
Front: OIL / OF / GLADNESS
Side: JUSTIN GATES
Re: SACRAMENTO

RECT., SMOOTH BASE, 6" and 5"
APPLIED TOP
AQUA, 6", $110.00- 2002
AQUA, 5", $230.00- 2011
Note: LABEL AT RIGHT was TRADE
MARKED in 1875. IN 1882 A.C.
TUFTS of SACRAMENTO BECAME
THE AGENT FOR THIS BRAND.

DR. A. LEPPER'S
ELECTRIC LIFE
FOR MAN AND BEAST!

SURE CURE!

INTERNAL AND EXTERNAL MEDICINE.

Headache and Earache in three minutes.

Toothache in one minute.

Neuralgia in five minutes.

Sprains in twenty minutes.

Sore Throat in ten minutes.

Colic and Cramps in five minutes.

Fever and Ague in one day.

Cholera and Cholera Morbus, Diarrhœa and Bloody Flux in one day.

Rheumatism in from one to thirty days.

Pain in the Back or Side in ten minutes.

Bad Coughs and Colds in one day.

Pleurisy in one day.

Deafness, Asthma, Piles, Bronchial Affections, Erysipelas, Palpitation of the Heart, Burns, Frosted Feet, Corns and Chilblains, Sore and Weak Eyes.

Catarrh in the Head and Throat.

Warranted to Cure or No Pay.

COUGHS AND COLDS.—Take a teaspoonful in a little sugar and water three times a day, and bathe the breast night and morning with the medicine.

NERVOUS HEADACHE.—Rub a little on your hands and inhale freely. Bathe the head and temples freely until the pain ceases.

SICK HEADACHE.—Take inwardly one teaspoonful in a wineglass of water, and apply as for Nervous Headache.

SORE THROAT.—Take one teaspoonful in a little water, gargle and swallow, and bathe outside.

TOOTHACHE.—Put a teaspoonful in the mouth and run over the tooth, and apply to the face and jaw until relieved.

COLIC AND CRAMPS.—Take internally one teaspoonful in warm water, and bathe the stomach and bowels freely with the medicine.

NEURALGIA AND SPINAL AFFECTIONS.—Bathe immediately over the part affected, and inhale freely until relieved.

EARACHE.—Put one or two drops in the ear, and bathe around the ear for a few minutes.

SORE AND WEAK EYES.—Close the eyes and bathe around them, and avoid getting any of the solution in the eyes; keep the eyes closed until the sensation has passed. No article equals this medicine for the eyes and ears.

RHEUMATISM.—Bathe very freely until the pain is all gone, then apply it morning and night for three or four days. Use the medicine inwardly—a teaspoonful in a wineglass of water night and morning for several days.

DIARRHŒA AND DYSENTERY.—Same as for Colic and Cramps.

SABER, BAYONET, GUNSHOT AND OTHER WOUNDS.—Apply a bandage and occasionally bathe with the medicine.

SPRAINS, BRUISES, ETC.—The same as for Wounds.

BURNS, SCALDS, ETC.—Dilute the medicine, saturate cotton with it and apply.

FEVER AND AGUE.—One teaspoonful three times a day, before meals, in water.

PLEURISY.—A teaspoonful three times a day, and bathe the side freely night and morning with it.

INFLAMMATION OF THE KIDNEYS.—Take one teaspoonful every morning and night in a wineglass of water for four or five days, bathing the back immediately over the kidneys with the same medicine night and morning.

LIVER COMPLAINT AND PALPITATION OF THE HEART.—Take internally one teaspoonful in a wineglass of water morning and evening for twelve days, and bathe freely the breast and left side morning and evening.

DEAFNESS.—From one to five drops in the ear, and bathe around the ear morning and night for several days.

PILES.—Take internally one teaspoonful in a wineglass of water night and morning for four or five days, and apply with the fingers diluted one-half water every operation.

ERYSIPELAS.—Take inwardly one teaspoonful morning and night for four five days, bathing the parts affected three or four times a day for five days.

DYSPEPSIA.—Take internally one teaspoonful morning and night for twelve days. Bathe the breast and left side with the same.

Front: **DR. LEPPER'S / ELECTRIC LIFE**

RECT., SMOOTH BASE, 6" and 7 ½"
AQUA, 6", $60.00- 2001
AQUA, 7 ½", 150.00- 2017
COMMON in the SMALL SIZE
SCARCE in the LARGER SIZE
Varient: **MISSPELLED 'LEPPEPS'**
Locale: **SACRAMENTO, CAL.**

Front: **DR. LEPPER's / ELECTRIC / LIFE**

    RECT., SMOOTH BASE, 8" and 5 ¾"
    TOOLED TOP
    AQUA, 5 ¾", $180.00- 2017
    BOTH SIZES are SCARCE

Front: **DR. LEPPER'S / MOUNTAIN / TEA**

    RECT., SMOOTH BASE, 6 ¼" and 8 ½"
    APPLIED and TOOLED TOP
    AQUA, 8 ½", T.T. with LABEL, $325.00- 2017
    COMMON in the SMALL SIZE
    SCARCE in the LARGE SIZE
    RARE WITH an APPLIED TOP

Front: **LIEBIG'S DISPENSARY / 400 GEARY ST. S.F.**

    RECT., SMOOTH BASE, 7 ¾"
    TOOLED TOP
    AQUA, $60.00- 2017
    SCARCE

Front: **DR. LIEBIG'S / GERMAN INVIGORATOR / 400 GEARY ST. S.F.**

    RECT., SMOOTH BASE, 6 ¾" and 8 ¼"
    TOOLED TOP
    AMBER, 6 ¾", $140.00- 2017
    COMMON in the SMALL SIZE
    SCARCE in the LARGE SIZE

Front: **LIEBIG'S DISPENSARY / FOR DISEASES OF MEN / 400 GEARY ST. S.F. CAL.**

    RECT., SMOOTH BASE, 8"
    TOOLED TOP
    AQUA
    SCARCE

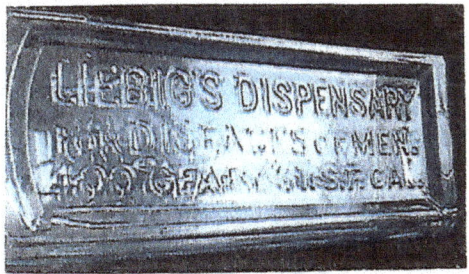

Front: **DR. LIEBIG'S WONDERFUL / GERMAN INVIGORATOR NO.1 / 400 GEARY ST. S.F. CAL.**

    RECT., SMOOTH BASE, 7 ¾"
    APPLIED and TOOLED TOP
    AQUA, APPLIED TOP, $200.00- 1995
    SCARCE WITH a TOOLED TOP
    RARE WITH APPLIED TOP
    Varient: 'NO. 2', $50.00- 2017
        RARE, AQUA with a TOOLED TOP

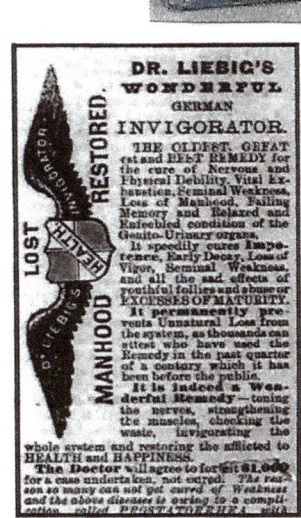

Front: LEVING'S / HOARHOUND AND / ELECAMPANE

    RECT., SMOOTH BASE, 6 ½"
    TOOLED TOP
    AQUA
    RARE
    Locale: SAN FRANCISCO
    Note: LABEL TRADE MARKED in 1892 BY
          O.K. LEVINGS of S.F.

Side: LEVING'S
Front: HOARHOUND / AND / ELECAMPANE
Side: SYRUP

    RECT., SMOOTH BASE, 7"
    APPLIED and TOOLED TOP
    GREEN
    AQUA, APPLIED TOP, $400.00- 2006
    AQUA, APPLIED TOP, $170.00- 2017 (flake)
    EX. RARE in ALL VARIENTS
    Note: HAS THE WESTERN CURVED R's

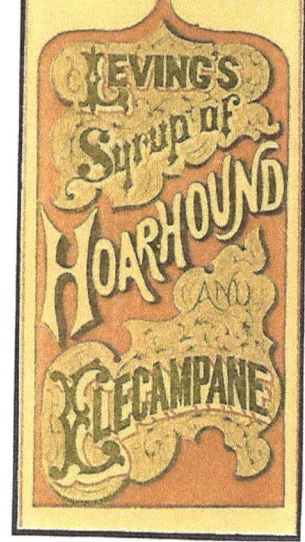

Side: DR. A.M. LORYEA & CO.
Front: UNKWEED REMEDY / RHEUMATIC
       CURE
Side: OREGON

    RECT., SMOOTH BASE, 8"
    APPLIED TOP
    AQUA, $3500.00- 2006
    EX. RARE

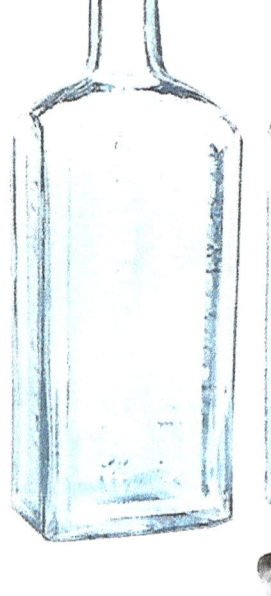

Front: LULL'S / ANTI SPASMODOC / FOR
       COUGHS / SAN FRANCISCO / CAL.

    RECT., SMOOTH BASE, 4 ½"
    TOOLED TOP
    AQUA, $100.00- 1996
    RARE

Front: M.A.C. / FOR DYSPEPSIA / AND
       CONSTIPATION / SMITH BROS. /
       FRESNO, CAL.
Side: FOR SEA – SICKNESS
Side FOR TRAIN – SICKNESS

    RECT., SMOOTH BASE, 8 ½" and 6 ¾"
    TOOLED TOP
    CLEAR, 8 ½", $40.00- 2017
    BOTH SIZES are COMMON

Front: McBURNEY'S / KIDNEY & BLADDER
       CURE / LOS ANGELES, CAL.

    RECT., SMOOTH BASE, 5"
    TOOLED TOP
    CLEAR
    SCARCE

Front: A.M. McBOYLE / SAN FRANCISCO
Re: PRATT'S / ABOLITION OIL

    RECT., SMOOTH BASE, 6 ¾"
    TOOLED TOP
    AQUA
    EX. RARE

Front: DR. / J.J. McBRIDE
Re: KING OF PAIN

    RECT., SMOOTH BASE, 6"
    APPLIED and TOOLED TOP
    DEEP AQUA, A.T., $210.00- 2017
    COMMON in AQUA
    EX. RARE in LIME GREEN
    Note: AD CIRCA 1881

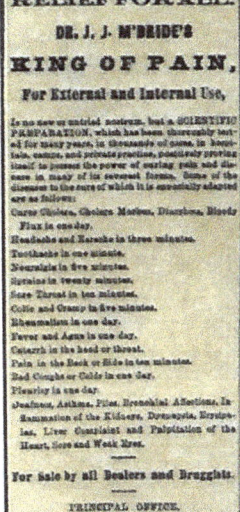

Front: DR. McBRIDE
Side: WORLD'S RELIEF
Side: WORLD'S RELIEF

    RECT., SMOOTH BASE, 6 ½"
    APPLIED TOP
    AQUA, $250.00- 2017
    RARE
    Note: HAS THE WESTERN CURVED R's,
         AD CIRCA 1875.

Front: A.M. McBOYLE & CO. /
       SAN FRANCISCO
Re: PRATT'S / NEW LIFE

    RECT., SMOOTH BASE, 7 ½"
    APPLIED TOP
    AQUA, $375.00- 2017
    RARE

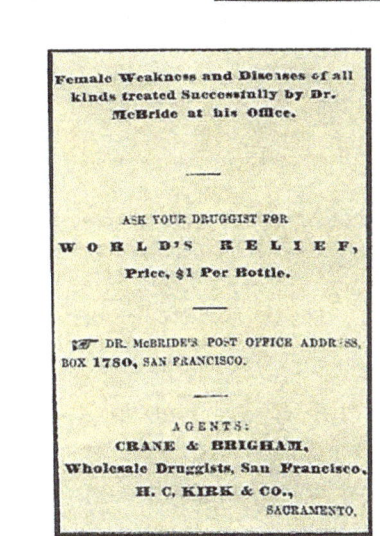

Side: McCLELLAN'S
Front: DIPHTHERIA
Side: REMEDY

    RECT., SMOOTH BASE, 7 ¾"
    APPLIED and TOOLED TOP
    AQUA
    CLEAR FLINT GLASS, T.T.,
            $90.00- 2003
    RARE with APPLIED TOP
    SCARCE with TOOLED TOP

Front: COMPOUND / FLUID EXTRACT / OF
        MANZANITA / DRS. McDONALD
        & LEVY / SACRAMENTO CITY /
        CALIFORNIA

    OVAL, OPEN PONTIL, 4 ½"
    ROLLED LIP
    AQUA, $1800.00- 1994
           $400.00- 2000 (crack)
    RARE
    CIRCA: 1853
    Note: ADS are CIRCA 1854 and THE LITHO
    OF McDONALD'S DRUG STORE IS
    CIRCA 1850's. THIS IS ONE OF THE
    WESTERN FRONTIER EARLIEST
    EMBOSSED BOTTLES.

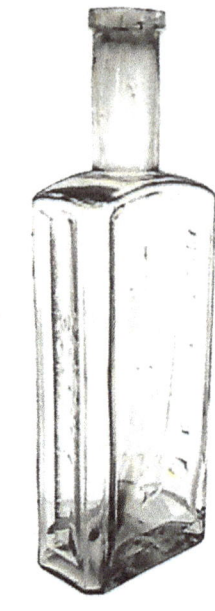
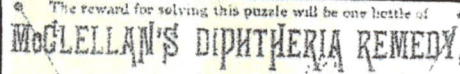
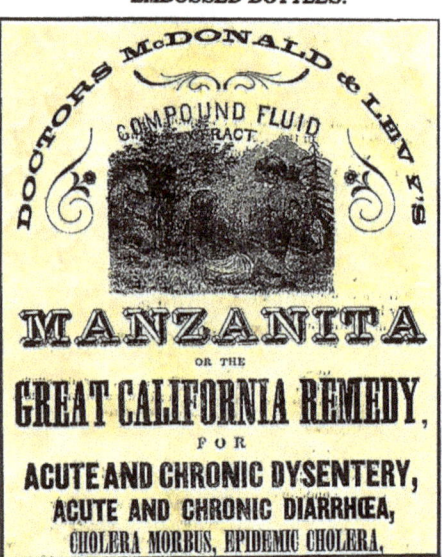

Front: MEYER'S COUGH REMEDY / MAN'F BY / GIANT
MEDICINE CO. / HELENA, MONT.

RECT., SMOOTH BASE, 6 ½"
TOOLED TOP
AQUA, $180.00- 2017
RARE

Side: DR. MINTIE'S
Front: NEPHRETICUM
Side: SAN FRANCISCO

RECT., SMOOTH BASE, 7"
APPLIED and TOOLED TOP
AQUA, A.T., $400.00- 2017
RARE
Note: HAS THE WESTERN CURVED R's,
LABEL was TRADE MARKED in 1877
BY A.E. MINTIE of S.F. ADS are
CIRCA 1878.

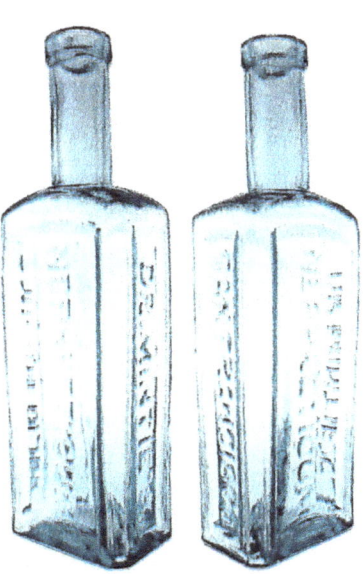

Front: MOORE'S / REVEALED / monogram / REMEDY

OVAL, SMOOTH BASE, 8"
APPLIED and TOOLED TOP
AMBER
COMMON with TOOLED TOP
RARE with APPLIED TOP
Locale: SEATTLE, W.T.

Front: **DR. MOTT'S / WILD CHERRY TONIC / SPRUANCE, STANLEY & CO.**

    SQUARE, SMOOTH BASE, 9"
    APPLIED TOP
    AMBER, $725.00- 1995
    EX . RARE
    CIRCA: 1881
    Locale: SAN FRANCISCO

Front: **DR. MOTT'S / WILD CHERRY TONIC / A.H. POWERS & CO.**

    SQUARE, SMOOTH BASE, 9"
    APPLIED TOP
    AMBER, $450.00- 2014
    RARE
    Locale: SACRAMENTO, CAL.
    Note: LABEL TRADE MARKED in 1877 by
          POWERS & HENDERSON, SAC.

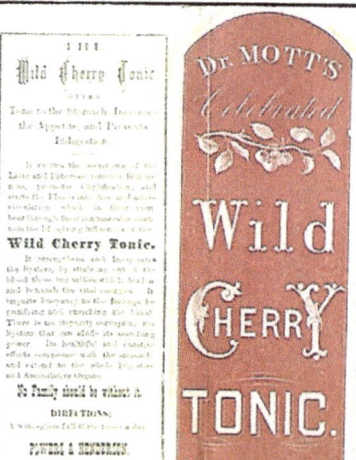

Front: **DR. MURRAYS' / MAGIC OIL / S.F. CAL.**

    RECT., SMOOTH BASE, 7 ¼" and 6 ¼"
    APPLIED and TOOLED TOP
    AQUA, A.T., 6 ¼", $600.00- 2017
    AMETHYST, T.T., 6 ¼", $110.00- 1998
    RARE in AQUA
    EX . RARE in LIME GREEN and AMETHYST
    Varient: HAS a RING NECK WITH A
           TOOLED TOP, AQUA, EX. RARE

Side: **NICHOL'S / INJECTION**

    RECT., SMOOTH BASE, 7 ¾"
    APPLIED TOP
    COBALT
    AQUA, $110.00- 2009
    SCARCE
    Note: ONE SIDE HAS AN INDENT FOR A
          SYRINGE., HAS THE FAT, FLAT
          EMOSSING FONT, SIMILAR TO OTHER
          WESTERN BLOWN BOTTLES.
    Varient: NICHOL'S / INFALLABLE / INJECTION

Front: MOON'S BLOOD POISON REMEDY /
/ PREPARED BY / JESSE H. MOON /
RITZVILLE, WASH.

RECT., SMOOTH BASE, 6"
TOOLED TOP
CLEAR
EX. RARE

Front: NATIONAL / HORSE LINIMENT

RECT., SMOOTH BASE, 7 ½" and 5 ½"
TOOLED TOP
AQUA, 5 ½", T.T., $60.00- 2017
BOTH SIZES are SCARCE
Note: AD FROM 1895, AND AN EARLY
   TRADE CARD ADVERTISING ANOTHER
   OF JOHN R. WILLIAMS PRODUCTS.

Front: NEUROTINE / MANUFACTURING
   CO. S.F.

RECT., SMOOTH BASE, 6"
TOOLED TOP
AQUA
EX. RARE
Note: LABEL TRADE MARKED in 1884 by
   JOHN MacLENNAN of S.F.

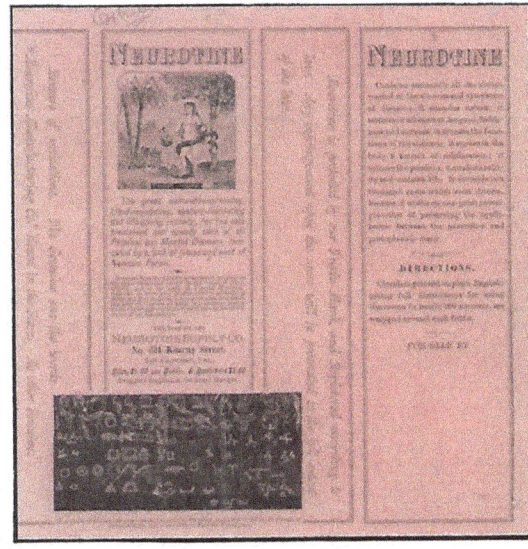

Side: NEWELL'S
Front: PULMONARY / SYRUP
Side: REDINGTON & CO.

RECT., SMOOTH BASE, 7 ¼"
APPLIED and TOOLED TOP
AQUA, A.T., $20.00- 2017
COMMON in AQUA
EX. RARE in GREEN
Varient: REDINGTON is SLUGGED OUT
Note: AD AT RIGHT is CIRCA 1868

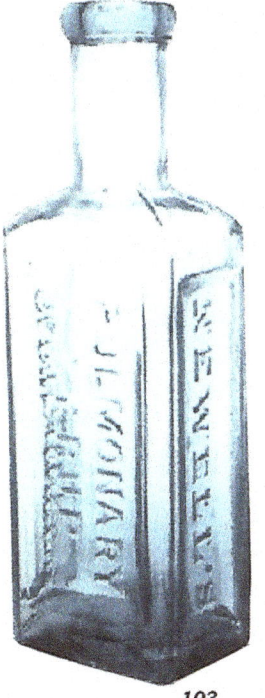

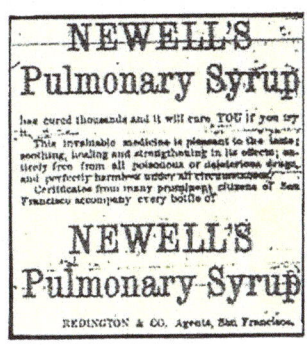

Front: NELSON'S EXTRACT OF / ROSES & ROSEMARY / H.P. WAKELEE AGENT

RECT., SMOOTH BASE, 7" and 8"
APPLIED TOP
SAPPHIRE BLUE, 7", $180.00- 2017
SMALL SIZE is SCARCE
LARGE SIZE is RARE
Note: BOTTLE is BELIEVED TO BE ENGLISH
   BLOWN. TRADE MARKED in 1870
   BY H.P. WAKELEE S.F.

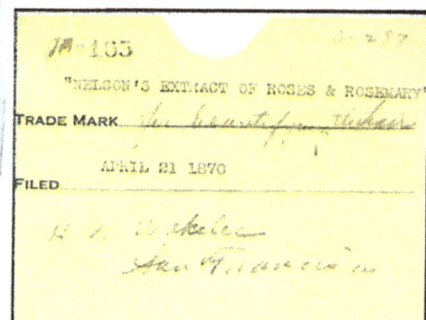

Front: NONE GENUINE / WITHOUT THIS / TRADE MARK / man and serpent

RECT., SMOOTH BASE, 9" and 10"
TOOLED TOP
AQUA
AMBER, 9", $160.00- 2015
RARE in AMBER
EX. RARE in AQUA

Front: DR. A.M.NOXON / IDAHO SPRING'S, COL.

SQUARE, SMOOTH BASE, 8 ¾"
APPLIED TOP
AMBER
EX. RARE
CIRCA: 1885

Front: OREGON / baby / BLOOD / PURIFIER / WM PFUNDER & CO. / PORTLAND, OR.

RECT., SMOOTH BASE, 6" and 7 ¾"
TOOLED TOP
AQUA
CLEAR, $130.00- 2006
AMBER, $110.00- 2007
COMMON in AMBER
RARE in CLEAR and AQUA

Front: OREGON / KIDNEY / TEA

    OVAL, SMOOTH BASE, 9"
    TOOLED TOP
    AMBER
    RARE
    Note: A DR. HENLEY PRODUCT, LABEL TRADE MARKED
       IN 1880. ALSO AT RIGHT IS AN EASTERN DISTRIBUTED
       VARIENT FROM THE STARK MEDICINE CO. N.Y.

Base: PACIFIC GLASS WORKS

    ROUND, SMOOTH BASE, 6' and 7"
    APPLIED TOP
    GREEN
    AQUA, 7", $70.00- 2017
    LT. BLUE, 7", $190.00- 2017
    ALL VARIENTS are RARE

Front: PALA VERDE BALSAM

    SQUARE, SMOOTH BASE, 8 ¾"
    APPLIED TOP
    AMBER, $110.00- 1995
    RARE

Front: P.P.M. CO.

    RECT., SMOOTH BASE, 7 ½"
    APPLIED TOP
    AQUA
    EX. RARE
    Note: USED BY THE PACIFIC PROPRIETARY
          MEDICINE CO. S.F, MOST LIKELY IN
          THE 1870's.

Side: PARADISE OIL
Side: PARADISE OIL

    RECT., SMOOTH BASE, 6"
    TOOLED TOP
    AQUA, $80.00- 1997
    SCARCE
    Note: NO PIC AVAILABLE

Front: INDIAN / TRA – QUILLAUGH'S /
       BALSAM / DR. R. PARKER S.F.

    ROUND, SMOOTH BASE, 8 ½"
    APPLIED TOP
    GREEN
    COPPER PUCE, $21,000.00- 2015
    EX. RARE
    Note: ONE of THE FIRST BOTTLES
    BLOWN AT THE S.F. GLASS WORKS.
    LABEL TRADE MARKED in 1865 by
    RALZEMOND PARKER S.F. ADS ARE
    ALSO CIRCA 1865.

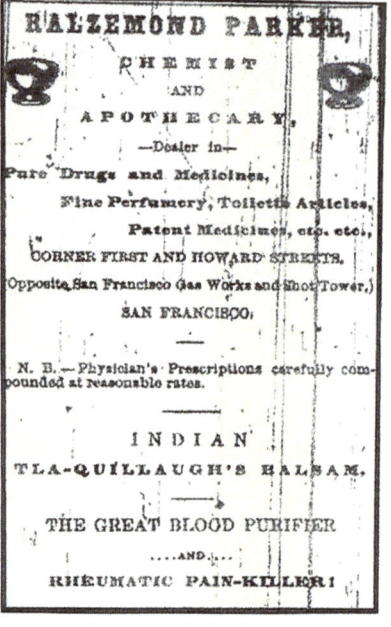

Front: DR. PAREIRA'S
Re: ITALIAN REMEDY

    RECT., OPEN PONTIL, 5"
    APPLIED TOP
    AQUA
    EX. RARE
    Note: AD CIRCA 1859. THE WESTERN
    AGENT FOR THIS BRAND WAS DR. J.
    PERRAULT of S.F. SEE AD at RIGHT.

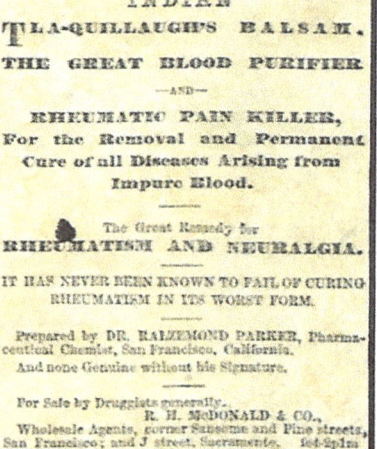

Front: PAWNEE / INDIAN BALM

    RECT., SMOOTH BASE, 4 ½"
    TOOLED TOP
    CLEAR
    SCARCE
    Varient: PAIN BALM

Side: DR. PETTI'S
Front: AUSTRALIAN / BLOOD
Side: PURIFIER

    RECT., SMOOTH BASE, 8 ¼"
    APPLIED TOP
    AQUA
    EX. RARE
    Locale: SAN FRANCISCO

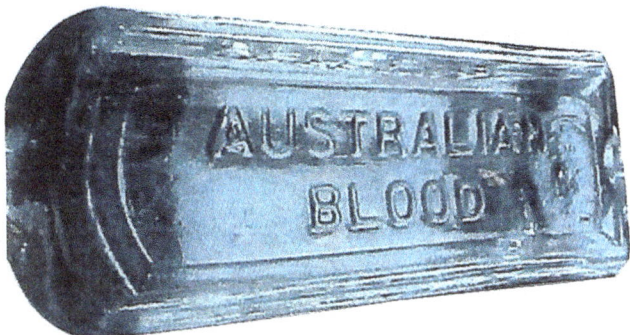
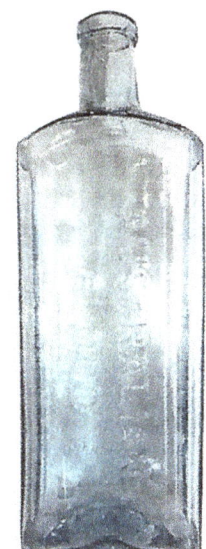

Front: PAWNEE INDIAN / TOO – REE

    RECT., SMOOTH BASE, 7 ¾" and 6 ¼"
    TOOLED TOP
    AQUA
    COMMON in BOTH SIZES
    Varient: FLAT FRONT and BACK
       CLEAR, 7 ½", T.T., $50.00- 2017
    Note: AD FROM 1891 S.F. DIRECTORY.

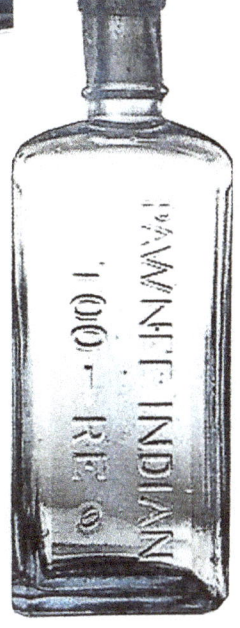
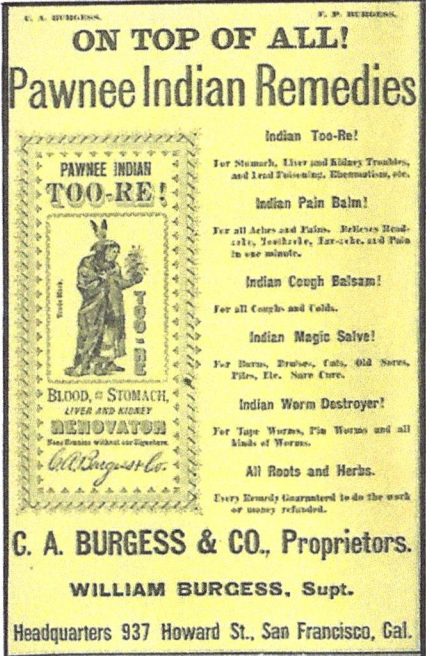

Side: CHRETIEN PFEISTER / SAN FRANCISCO
Side: TRICOMALICUM

RECT., SMOOTH BASE, 5 ½" and 6"
APPLIED and TOOLED TOP
AQUA and CLEAR
ALL VARIENTS are EX. RARE

Front: DR. PERRY'S / LAST CHANCE
Re: LINIMENT

RECT., SMOOTH BASE, 5 ¾"
APPLIED TOP
AQUA, $250.00- 2017
SCARCE
Note: AD CIRCA 1872

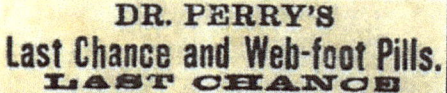

Front: PFUNDER'S / baby / TRADE MARK /
COPYRIGHT SECURED / SSS /
FEVER and AGUE / MIXTURE

RECT., SMOOTH BASE, 6"
TOOLED TOP
AMBER, $500.00- 2006
RARE
Locale: PORTLAND, ORE.

Front: WM. PFUNDER / OREGON / No. 7133 /
baby / TRADE MARK / REGISTERED /
MARCH 23rd 1879 / BLOOD PURIFIER /
WM. PFUNDER & CO. / PORTLAND, ORE.

RECT., SMOOTH BASE, 6
TOOLED TOP
AMBER
SCARCE
Note: EARLY AD and TRADE CARDS BELOW.

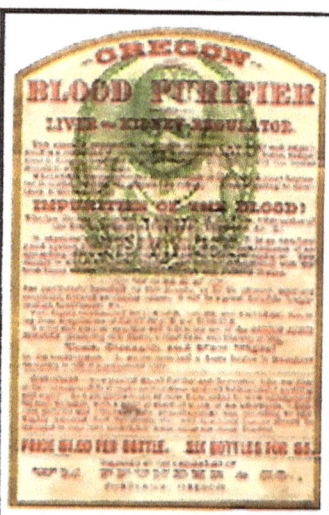

108

Front: DR. J.E. PLOUF'S / RHEUMATISM CURE

    RECT., SMOOTH BASE, 6 ½"
    CLEAR
    RARE
    Locale: SAN FRANCISCO

Front: PRATT'S / ABOLITION OIL
Re: FOR ABOLISHING PAIN

    RECT., SMOOTH BASE, 5 ¾"
    APPLIED, TOOLED and FLAIR TOP
    AQUA, A.T., $60.00- 2019
    DEEP AQUA, FLAIR TOP, $425.00- 2010
    AQUA, EARLY T.T., $130.00- 2017
    COMMON in AQUA
    EX. RARE in GREEN
    Varient: BACKWARDS 'S' in ABOLISHING,
              AQUA, A.T., $110.00- 2019
    Note: THERE IS ALSO A BROKEN
       SPECIMEN in COBALT BLUE THAT IS
       A BIGGER SIZE, WITH A FOOTPRINT OF
       1 ½" x 2 ½".
    AD CIRCA 1869.

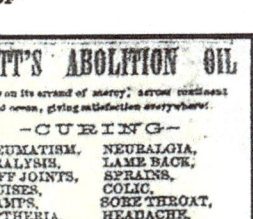

Front: PRATT'S / NEW LIFE
Side: A. McBOYLE & CO.
Side: SAN FRANCISCO

    RECT., SMOOTH BASE, 8"
    APPLIED TOP
    AQUA
    DEEP PUCE
    YELLOW OLIVE, $550.00- 2006
    AMBER, $475.00- 2010
    ALL COLORS are RARE
    Note: AD CIRCA 1869

Front: PRATT'S / NEW LIFE

    RECT., SMOOTH BASE, 8 ¼"
    APPLIED TOP
    COBALT, $5500.00- 2002
    EX. RARE

Front: POND'S / MONARCH / LINIMENT

    RECT., SMOOTH BASE, 6 ½"
    TOOLED TOP
    AQUA
    RARE
    Locale: HOLLISTER, CAL.

Front: POND'S / COMPOUND / SYRUP OF FIGS

    RECT., SMOOTH BASE, 6 ½"
    TOOLED TOP
    AQUA
    RARE
    Locale: HOLLISTER, CAL.

Side: RENNE'S
Side: NERVINE

    RECT., SMOOTH BASE, 5 ½"
    APPLIED TOP
    AQUA
    SCARCE
    Locale: COLORADO SPRINGS, COLO.

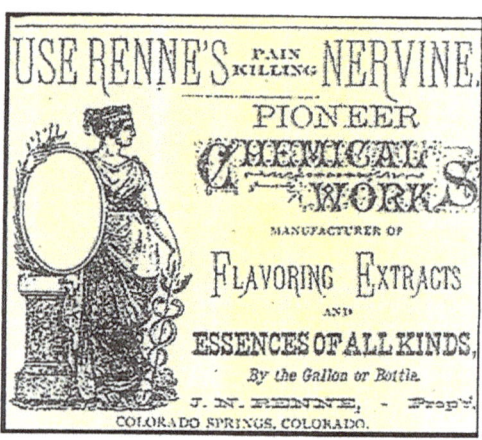

Front: GOLDEN BALSAM / RICHARD'S / SAN FRANCISCO

    ROUND, SMOOTH BASE, 5 ½"
    APPLIED and TOOLED TOP
    AQUA, $30.00- 2017
    DEEP AQUA, $275.00- 2015
    COMMON
    Note: LABEL TRADE MARKED in 1865
          BY C. FRENCH RICHARDS, S.F.

Front: INJECTION RICORD / PARIS

    SQUARE, SMOOTH BASE, 6"
    APPLIED TOP
    COBALT, $160.00- 2017
    RARE
    Note: AD IS CIRCA 1877 and ENDS ANY
          ARGUMENT ABOUT THE LOCALE
          OF THIS BOTTLE E.B. JORGENSEN
          OF S.F. WAS THE WESTERN AGENT.

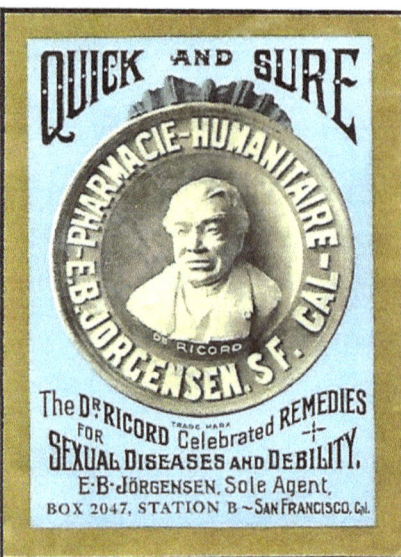
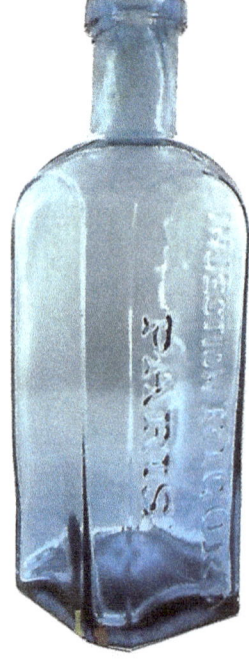

Side: DR. ROWELL'S
Side: FIRE OF LIFE
Front: BURNETT AND CO. / APOTHECARY / NO. 327 MONTGOMERY ST. / SAN FRANCISCO

RECT., SMOOTH BASE, 6"
TOOLED TOP
AQUA, $300.00- 2010
Note: DR. CHAS. ROWELL TRADE MARKED THIS LABEL in 1883. G.G. BURNETT WAS THE AGENT FROM 1875 – 1897.

Front: ROWLER'S / RHEUMATISM MEDICINE / PREPARED BY / DR. J.R. BOYCE / SACRAMENTO

ROUND, OPEN PONTIL and SMOOTH BASE, 7 ¾"
APPLIED TOP
LT. GREEN, S.B., $2000.00- 2014
AQUA, O.P., $3800.00- 1997
EX. RARE
Note: ADS CIRCA 1860

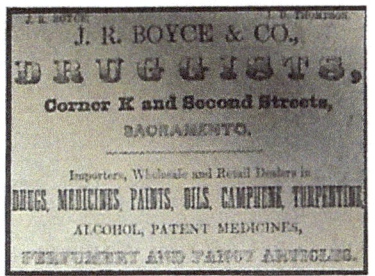

Side: FRED SANDELIN
Front: SWEDISH / DYSPEPSIA CURE
Side: OAKLAND, CAL.

RECT., SMOOTH BASE, 9"
TOOLED TOP
AQUA
RARE
Note: TRADE MAEKED In 1882 by C.F. SANDELIN, OAKLAND.

Side: S. & CO. BLOOD
Side: PURIFIER

    RECT., SMOOTH BASE, 8 ½"
    APPLIED TOP
    AQUA, $700.00- 1998
    BLUE, $475.00- 2017 (chip)
          $1300.00- 2003
    RARE in AQUA
    EX. RARE in SHADES of BLUE
    Note: A PRODUCT of J.G. STEELE,
        SAN FRANCISCO

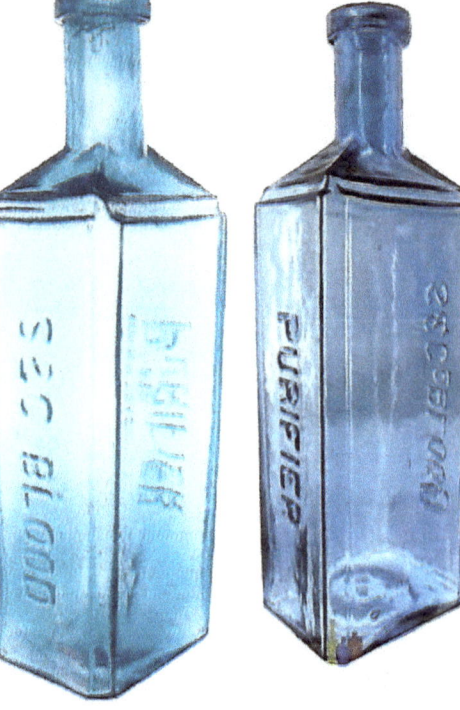

Front: SHAW'S / GLYCERINE / LOTION

    RECT., SMOOTH BASE, 5"
    TOOLED TOP
    AQUA
    SCARCE
    Locale: SAN FRANCISCO

Front: SILVER STATE / OVERLAND LINIMENT

    RECT., SMOOTH BASE, 7 ¼"
    TOOLED TOP
    AQUA
    RARE
    Locale: BUTTE, MONTANA

Front: MAGIC COUGH SYRUP / PREPARED
         BY / J.B. SCOTT / SALINAS, CAL.

    RECT., SMOOTH BASE, 6"
    TOOLED TOP
    AQUA, $70.00- 2017
    RARE

Side: DR. BARLOW J. SMITH'S
Side: CALORIC VITA OIL

    RECT., SMOOTH BASE, 5 ¾"
    TOOLED TOP
    AQUA
    SCARCE
    CIRCA: 1882
    Locale: SAN FRANCISCO
    Note: LABEL WAS TRADE MARKED in
        1881 by DR. BARLOW SMITH S.F.

Front: **JOHN F. SNOW'S / VICTORY**

    OVAL, SMOOTH BASE, 6"
    APPLIED TOP
    AQUA, and GREEN
    EX. RARE
    CIRCA: 1872
    Note: AD is CIRCA 1874 FROM THE S.F.
          DIRECTORY, THIS BOTTLE PROBABLY
          CONTAINED a DYE or POLISH.

Front: **THE SPECIFIC / A NO. 1 / A SELF CURE / TRADE MARK**

    RECT., SMOOTH BASE, 5"
    TOOLED TOP
    AQUA
    SCARCE
    Note: LABEL TRADE MARKED in 1887 by
          A. SCHOENHEIT of SAN JOSE CAL.

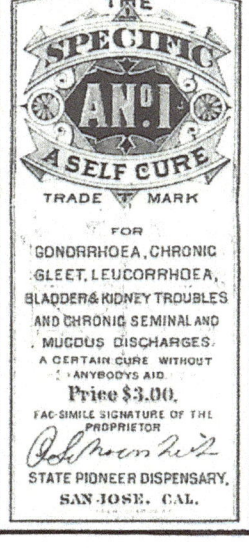

Front: **M. SPOONHAUER'S / mortar and pestle / BLOOD PURIFIER**

    RECT., SMOOTH BASE, 7"
    TOOLED TOP
    CLEAR
    RARE
    Locale: DENVER, COLO.

Front: **S.I. / monogram**
Side: **THE STANDARD TONIC**
Side: **SHERRY & IRON**
Re: **THE SHERRY & IRON CO. / STOCKTON, CAL. USA**

    TAPERED SQUARE, SMOOTH BASE
    APPLIED & TOOLED TOP, 11"
    YELLOW AMBER, A.T., $2200.00- 2017
    RARE in AQUA
    EX. RARE in SHADES of AMBER

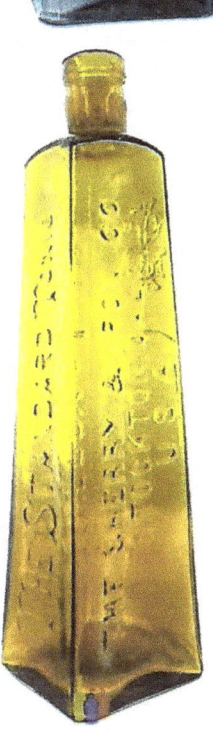

Front: **STARK'S / CATARRH / INHALENT**

    RECT., SMOOTH BASE, 2 ¾"
    TOOLED TOP
    AQUA
    RARE
    Note: HAS WESTERN CURVED R's

Front: **V. SQUARZA**

ROUND, SMOOTH BASE, 8 ½"
APPLIED TOP
COBALT, $8000.00- 2002
EX. RARE
Locale: SAN FRANCISCO
Note: LABELS TRADE MARKED in
1864 and 1865.

Side: **SUCH'S**
Front: **CALIFORNIA CURE / FOR ASTHMA**
Side: **& LUNG DISEASE**

RECT., SMOOTH BASE, 8"
APPLIED TOP
AQUA, $825.00- 1993
EX. RARE
Note: HAS WESTERN CURVED R's,
AD CIRCA 1874.

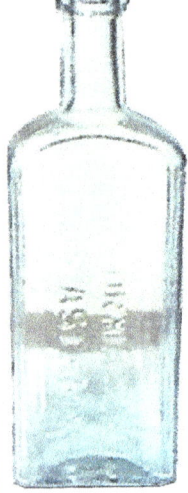

Front: STREAMER'S COUGH SYRUP / BOULDER, COLO.

RECT., SMOOTH BASE, 7 ½"
TOOLED TOP
AQUA
RARE

Side: W.R. STRONG
Front: DR. E.C. BALM
Side: SACRAMENTO

RECT., SMOOTH BASE, 4 ½"
TOOLED TOP
CLEAR FLINT GLASS and AQUA
EX. RARE
Note: HAS WESTERN CURVED R's,
AD is CIRCA 1867.
Varient: DR. E.C. BALM only.
HAS BOTH APPLIED and
TOOLED TOPS, AQUA.
THESE ARE SCARCE.

Front: mortar & pestle / SUN DRUG
CO. / LOS ANGELES

SQUARE, SMOOTH BASE, 8 ¾"
TOOLED TOP
AMBER, $250.00- 1993
RARE

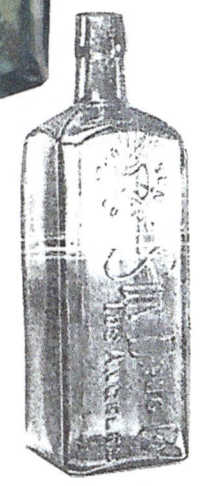

Side: SYRUP OF FIGS
Side: SYRUP OF FIGS

RECT., SMOOTH BASE, 6 ¾" and 7 ½"
TOOLED TOP
AQUA
COMMON
Note: THE EARLIEST VARIENT of THIS
BRAND is SHOWN AT THE RIGHT. IT
IS EMBOSSED ON THE SIDES ONLY.
CIRCA 1886 AND WAS FIRST SOLD
in RENO, NEVADA by W. PENNINGER
and R.E. QUEEN.
THERE ARE MANY EMBOSSING VARIENTS
OF THE LATER BOTTLES.
THEY ARE ALL COMMON.
TRADE CARD TO THE RIGHT.

Front: **4 STAR COUGH SYRUP / A.B. STEWART, SEATTLE**

    RECT., SMOOTH BASE, 6 ¾"
    TOOLED TOP
    AQUA
    EX. RARE
    CIRCA: 1886 – 1888

Front: **4 STAR COUGH SYRUP / STEWART & HOLMES DRUG CO. / SEATTLE, WASH.**

    RECT., SMOOTH BASE, 6 ¾"
    TOOLED TOP
    AQUA
    SCARCE
    CIRCA: 1890- 1900

Front: **DR. SIGNORETT'S COMP. EXT. / OF BUCHU / STEWART & HOLMES DRUG CO. / SEATTLE**

    RECT., SMOOTH BASE, 6 ¼"
    TOOLED TOP
    AQUA
    RARE
    CIRCA: 1890 – 1895

Front: **FIVE STAR LINIMENT / STEWART & HOLMES DRUG CO. / SEATTLE, TACOMA, WALLA WALLA**

    RECT., SMOOTH BASE, 7 ½"
    TOOLED TOP
    AQUA
    EX. RARE
    CIRCA: 1890

Front: **C.C.C. / COUGH CURE / STEWART & HOLMES DRUG CO. / WALLA WALLA, WASH.**

    RECT., SMOOTH BASE, 6 ¼"
    TOOLED TOP
    AQUA
    EX. RARE
    CIRCA: 1890 – 1892

Front: **DR. SIGNORETT'S / INFALLIBLE INJECTION / STEWART & HOLMES DRUG CO. SEATTLE**

    RECT., SMOOTH BASE, 7 ½"
    AQUA
    SCARCE
    SCARCE
    CIRCA: 1895

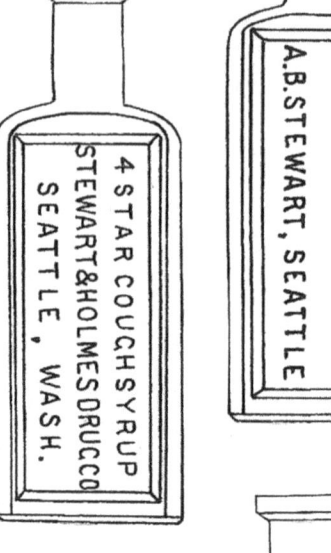
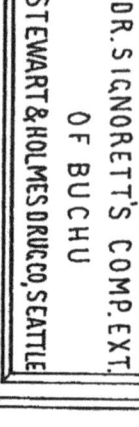
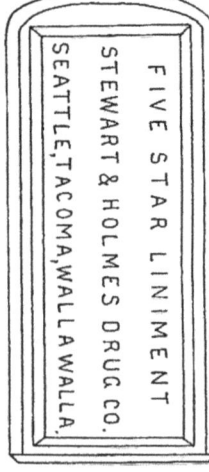
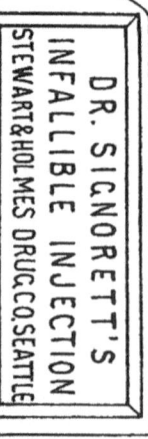

Front: **FOUR STAR / COUGH SYRUP / A.B. STEWART
& BRO. / TACOMA, WASH.**

    RECT., SMOOTH BASE, 6 ¾"
    TOOLED TOP
    AQUA
    EX. RARE
    CIRCA: 1887

Front: **SHATTUCK'S / FAMILY MEDICINES /
SPOKANE, WASH.**

    RECT., SMOOTH BASE, 6 ¾"
    TOOLED TOP
    CLEAR
    RARE
    CIRCA: 1905

Front: **TEMPLE of HEALTH**

    RECT., SMOOTH BASE, 9" and 7 ½"
    TOOLED TOP
    AQUA, 9", $160.00- 2009
    COMMON
    CIRCA: 1900

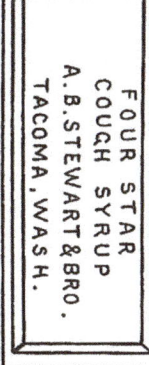

Front: **THAT WONDEROUS LINIMENT /
SAN JOSE, CAL.**
Side: **A. SCHOENHEIT**
Side: **STATE PIONEER DISPENSARY**

    RECT., SMOOTH BASE, 8" and 5 ½"
    TOOLED TOP
    AQUA, 8", $80.00- 2017
    COMMON
    Note: LABEL TRADE MARKED in 1883 by
          A. SCHOENHEIT, SAN JOSE, CAL

Front: **THOMPSON'S**
Re: **DANDELION AND CELERY /
TONIC**

    SQUARE, SMOOTH BASE, 9 ½"
    TOOLED TOP
    AMBER
    SCARCE

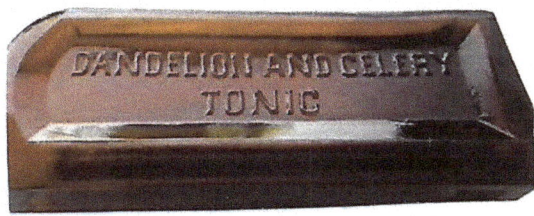

Front: **TIP TOP COUGH SYRUP**

    RECT., SMOOTH BASE, 6 ½"
    TOOLED TOP
    AQUA
    EX. RARE
    Locale: SAN DIEGO, CAL.
    Note: THIS BRAND WAS MANUFACTURED by
          WALTER LUTHER and SOLD by
          W.L. DODGE, DRUGGIST, of SAN
          DIEGO, CAL.

Front: **TOIYABE CHOLERA / AND / DIARRHOREA / REMEDY**

    RECT., SMOOTH BASE, 6"
    TOOLED TOP
    AQUA
    EX. RARE
    Locale: AUSTIN, NEVADA

Front: **TRADE TRIB MARK**
Re: **TRIB – A – LINIMENT FOR SPRAINS / BRUISES, BURNS, ETC. TRIB CO. / CARSON, NEVADA, SOLE OWNERS**

    SQUARE, SMOOTH BASE, 7 ¾"
    TOOLED TOP
    CLEAR
    EX. RARE

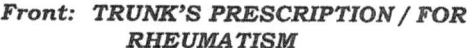

Front: **TRUNK'S PRESCRIPTION / FOR RHEUMATISM**

    RECT., SMOOTH BASE, 6 ½"
    TOOLED TOP
    CLEAR
    RARE
    Locale: DENVER, COLO.

Front: **TRUNK / BROS. / SYRUP / OIL OF PINE / COMPOUND / DENVER, COLO.**

    RECT., SMOOTH BASE, 6 ½"
    TOOLED TOP
    CLEAR
    RARE

Front: **UMATILLA / INDIAN RELIEF**

    RECT., SMOOTH BASE, 5 ¼"
    TOOLED TOP
    AQUA, $95.00- 1996
    RARE

Front: **TURNER'S / LIVER REGULATOR / TURNER BROS. / SAN FRANCISCO**

RECT., SMOOTH BASE, 7 ¾"
APPLIED TOP
AQUA
EX. RARE
Note: McMILLAN & KESTER WERE THE AGENTS FOR
TURNER BROS. PRODUCTS in the WEST.
EARLY TRADE CARD SHOWN BELOW.

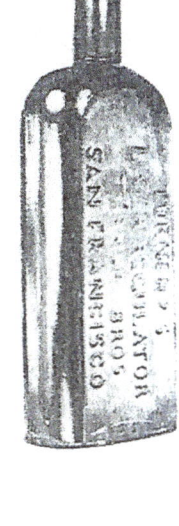

Front: **S.B. / DR. VANDERPOOL'S / HEADACHE AND LIVER CURE**

RECT., SMOOTH BASE, 8"
TOOLED TOP
AQUA, $90.00- 2017
RARE
Locale: DUFUR, OREGON

Front: **DR. VANDERPOOL'S / S.B. / COUGH & CONSUMPTION / CURE**

RECT., SMOOTH BASE, 6" and 5"
TOOLED TOP
AQUA
RARE
Locale: DUFUR, OREGON

Front: **VERMIN DESTROYER / PAT'D OCT. 8, 1872**

RECT., SMOOTH BASE, 4 ½"
APPLIED TOP
DEEP AQUA, $130.00- 1997
RARE
Note: PATENTED in 1872 by ELIZABETH HOOPER of
DIAMOND SPRINGS, EL DORADO CO., CAL.

Front: motif of a FISH with STAR
Side: TROUT OIL LINIMENT
Side: REMEDY NO. 2

    RECT., SMOOTH BASE, 6 ¼"
    APPLIED TOP
    AQUA, $800.00- 2008
    EX. RARE

Front: motif of a 'STAR' REMEDY / NO. 1
Side: ANTIBILIOUS CURE
Side: DR. VAN DYKE'S

    RECT., SMOOTH BASE, 6 ½"
    APPLIED TOP
    AQUA
    EX. RARE
    Note: BELOW is THE BACK OF A TRADE CARD. THE FRONT OF THE CARD HAS THE NAME H.H. JUDSON APOTHECARY, BUTTE AND KENTUCKY STS. THIS ADDRESS IS IN S.F. AND JUDSON WAS LISTED TO BE THERE in 1877. NOW FOR MORE CONFUSION, I FOUND THE TRADE MARK SHOWN, TO BE APPLIED FOR in 1878 by N. RICHARD of SAN FRANCISCO. ITS ANYBODYS GUESS WHERE THESE ARE ACTUALLY FROM, BUT ARE FOR SURE WESTERN BLOWN.

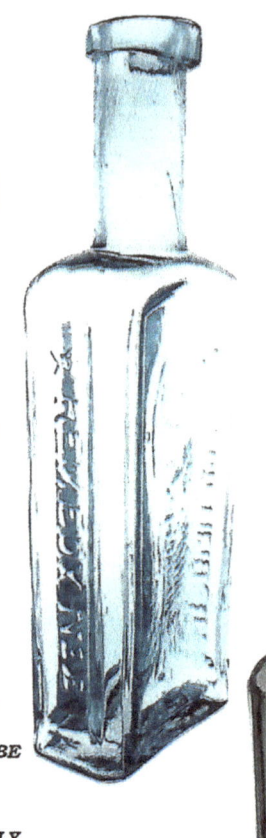

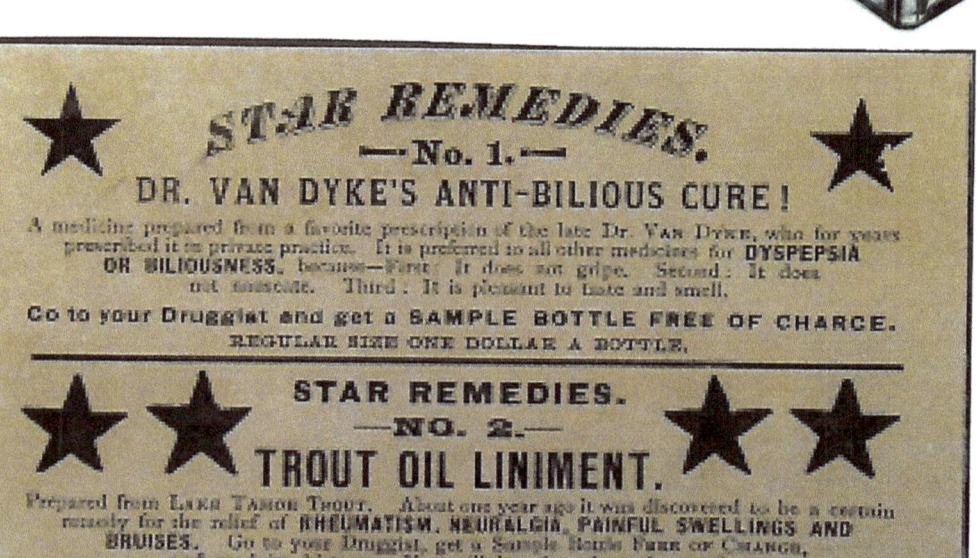

Front: DR. J.P.P. / VANDENBERGH'S
Re:　　WORM / SYRUP

　　RECT., SMOOTH BASE, 3 ¾"
　　ROLLED LIP
　　AQUA
　　EX. RARE
　　Note: HAS THE WESTERN CURVED R's.
　　　　LABEL at RIGHT WAS TRADE MARKED in
　　　　1870 by S.P.P. VANDENBERGH. of S.F.

Front: DR. S.P.P. / VANDENBERGH'S SR.
Re:　　WORM / SYRUP

　　RECT., SMOOTH BASE, 4"
　　TOOLED TOP
　　AQUA
　　EX. RARE
　　Note: HAS THE WESTERN CURVED R's.

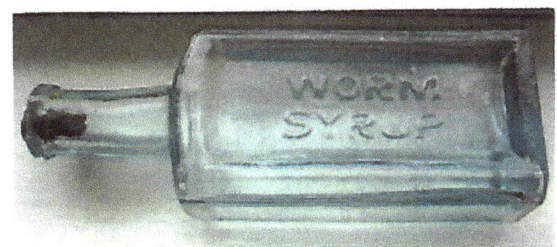

Front: VIGOR OF LIFE

　　RECT., SMOOTH BASE, 8" and 6 ¼"
　　TOOLED TOP
　　AQUA
　　COMMON
　　Note: LABEL TRADE MARKED in 1884 by
　　　　McCONKEY & CLARK, SACRAMENTO.
　　　　TRADE CARD CIRCA 1890.

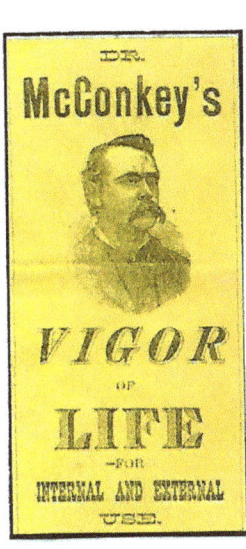

Side: DR. D.B. VINCENT'S
Front: MAGIC COUGH CURE
Side: SAN FRANCISCO

RECT., SMOOTH BASE, 7"
APPLIED and TOOLED TOP
AQUA, A.T., $1300.00- 2017
LIME GREEN
EX. RARE
Note: AD AT RIGHT is CIRCA 1869.
TOOLED TOP VARIENTS APPEAR
TO BE EASTERN BLOWN.

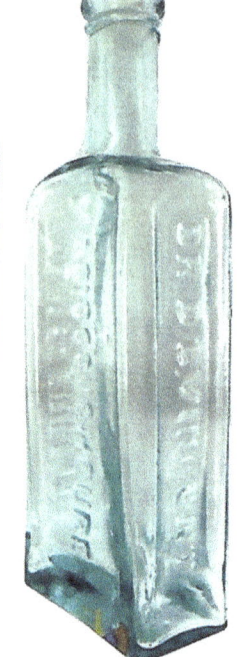
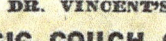

Side: DR. D.B. VINCENT'S
Front: ANGEL OF LIFE / FOR THE BLOOD
Side: SAN FRANCISCO

RECT., SMOOTH BASE, 8"
APPLIED TOP
AQUA, $1050.00- 1996
EX. RARE

Front: VIAVA / ROYAL
Re: MANUFACTURED BY / THE VIAVI
CO. / SAN FRANCISCO / CAL. USA

SQUARE, SMOOTH BASE, 8 ¼"
TOOLED TOP
AMBER
RARE
Note: CONTAINED A MEDICINAL TONIC.

Side: DR. WARREN'S
Front: BOTANIC / COUGH BALSAM
Side: S.F. CAL.

    RECT., SMOOTH BASE, 6 ¾" and 8 ½"
    APPLIED and TOOLED TOP
    AQUA, A.T., 8 ½", $275.00- 2017
    SCARCE with a TOOLED TOP
    RARE with an APPLIED TOP
    Note: HOMER WILLIAMS and ALFRED WRIGHT
         WERE THE AGENTS FOR THIS BRAND
         IN SAN FRANCISCO. HOMER WILLIAMS
         ALSO WAS THE SOLE OWNER OF THE
         YERBA BUENA BITTERS BRAND.

Front: WAIT'S WILD CHERRY TONIC
Re: THE GREAT TONIC

    SQUARE, SMOOTH BASE, 8 ¾"
    TOOLED TOP
    AMBER, $70.00- 2005
    COMMON
    Locale: SACRAMENTO

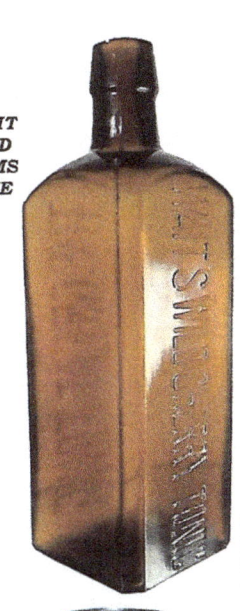

Front: GEO. Z. WAIT'S / MARVELOUS /
        REMEDY
Side: SACRAMENTO, CAL.

    RECT., SMOOTH BASE, 10"
    TOOLED TOP
    AQUA, $90.00- 2013
    RARE
    Note: LABEL at RIGHT was TRADE
         MARKED in 1895 by GEO. Z. WAIT.

Front: WEB'S / A NO. 1 / CATHARTIC /
        TONIC
Re: THE BEST / LIVER, KIDNEY &
        BLOOD / PURIFIER

    RECT., SMOOTH BASE, 9"
    TOOLED TOP
    AMBER, $90.00- 2017
    Locale: SACRAMENTO

Front: DR. WATSON'S LUNG BALSAM / M'F'G'D AT
TOOD'S PHARMACY / ABERDEEN, WASH.

RECT., SMOOTH BASE, 7 ¼"
TOOLED TOP
AQUA
EX. RARE
CIRCA: 1900

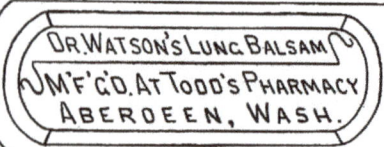

Front: DR. / WELCH'S
Re: INHALER / MEDICINE

3 SIDED, SMOOTH BASE, 2 ½"
TOOLED TOP
AQUA, $220.00- 2017
AMBER and COBALT
SCARCE in ALL COLORS.
Note: LABEL TRADE MARKED in
1891 by THE WELCH INHALER
AND MEDICINE CO. SAN JOSE.

Shoulder: ELECTRICITY IN A
          BOTTLE
Base: THE WEST ELECTRIC
          CURE CO.

ROUND, SMOOTH BASE, 2 ¾"
APPLIED TOP
COBALT
RARE
Locale: SAN FRANCISCO

Front: DR. H. WILLIAM'S
Side: MOUNTAIN PILLS
Side: GREENVILLE, CAL.

RECT., SMOOTH BASE, 2 ½"
TOOLED TOP
AQUA
RARE
CIRCA: 1882-1885

Front: WORNER'S / RATTLER OIL /
       PHOENIX, ARIZ.

RECT., SMOOTH BASE, 4 ½"
TOOLED TOP
CLEAR, $160.00- 1997
SCARCE

Side: **WHITE'S**
Front: **PRAIRIE FLOWER**
Side: **TOLEDO, O.**

RECT., SMOOTH BASE, 7"
APPLIED TOP
AQUA, $325.00- 2017
RARE
Note: BLOWN in SAN FRANCISCO and HAS THE WESTERN CURVED R's. CHANNING WHITE HAD AN OFFICE in BOTH SAN FRANCISCO and TOLEDO OHIO. TRADE CARD AT RIGHT PROVES THIS.

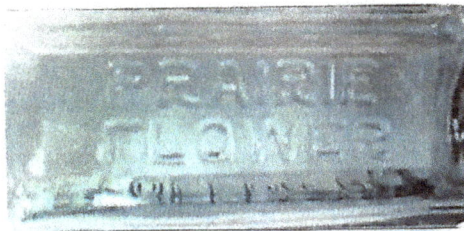

THEY ALL TAKE IT.

When the system is run down to that extent that you pass sleepless nights, are nervous and irritable, have gloomy forebodings, sour stomach, sick headache and coated tongue, do not enroll yourself as high private, in the rear rank, under General Debility, but cheer up and try

WHITE'S PRAIRIE FLOWER,

The Great Liver Panacea, now for sale in every city and town on the Continent. No medicine ever compounded is half its equal for the cure of

DYSPEPSIA & LIVER COMPLAINT

It has a specific power over the liver, and by curing the Liver, Dyspepsia and all other diseases arising from it, vanish as if by magic.

Sample bottles are sold at the small price of 25 cents that will convince you of its merit. Large size bottles 75 cents, for sale everywhere.

THE GREAT GERMAN REMEDY!
THE CELEBRATED
GERMAN ELIXIR

but recently introduced on the American Continent, has no equal in the world for the cure of

Throat and Lung Diseases, Consumption, Bronchitis, Bleeding of the Lungs; Coughs, Colds, &c.

A single trial will convince you of its great merit. It is rich in the medicinal properties of Tar, Wild Cherry, etc.

This valuable medicine is now sold in every City and Town on the Continent, at the low price of 25 cents for trial size. Large size bottles 75c. The directions are in full around each bottle. Be sure you get only German Elixir. The genuine bears the Prussian Coat of Arms, the fac-simile signature of Dr. Aug. Kaiser, and has his name blown on every 75c. bottle.

CHANNING WHITE,
PROPRIETOR,
TOLEDO, OHIO, and SAN FRANCISCO, CAL.

Front: **DR. A. ZAMBALDANO / COMPOUND SYRUP / OF EUCALYPTUS**

RECT., SMOOTH BASE, 6 ¾"
TOOLED TOP
AQUA and CLEAR
RARE
CIRCA: 1892

Front: YERBA SANTA (embossed in a CROSS)
Side: SAN FRANCISCO
Side: CALIFORNIA

RECT., SMOOTH BASE, 8 ½"
APPLIED and TOOLED TOP
DEEP AQUA, A.T., $450.00- 2013
LIME GREEN
RARE in AQUA
EX. RARE in GREEN
Varient: CROSS on BOTH FRONT and BACK
Note: FROM 1870-1877 THIS BRAND WAS DISTRIBUTED BY REDINGTON and HOSTETTER S.F. TRADE MARK WAS APPLIED FOR in 1870. IN 1877 TUFTS AND SPIEKER of SACRAMENTO BECAME THE SOLE AGENTS. THEY APPLIED FOR A TRADE MARK IN 1877.

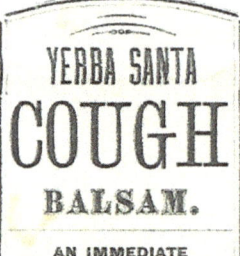
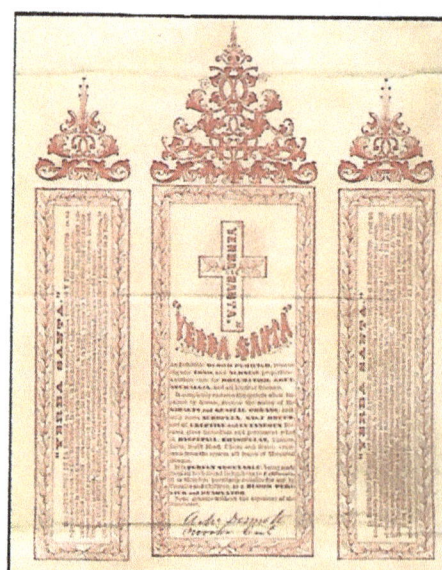

POT LIDS and OINTMENT POTS

Top: UNEQUALED / COLD / CREAM / FOR SOFTENING, BEAUTIFIYING / & PRESERVING THE SKIN / MADE BY / A.M. COLE / 88 SOUTH C STREET / VIRGINIA NEVADA

ROUND, CERAMIC POT LID. 2 ¾" ACROSS
CIRCA: 1878
RARE, $1100.00- 2018

Side: B. LEFEVRE & CO. / DRUGGISTS / SAN FRANCISCO

ROUND, CERAMIC POT, 3 ¼"
RARE

Side: B. LEFEVRE / APOTHECARY / 215 WASH. ST. / SAN FRANCISCO
(with mortar & pestle)

ROUND, CERAMIC POT
RARE
Note: LABEL BELOW WAS TRADE MARKED in 1878 BY LEFEVRE & KAHN. COULD THIS HAVE BEEN A LABEL ON ONE OF THE LIDS FOR THESE POTS.

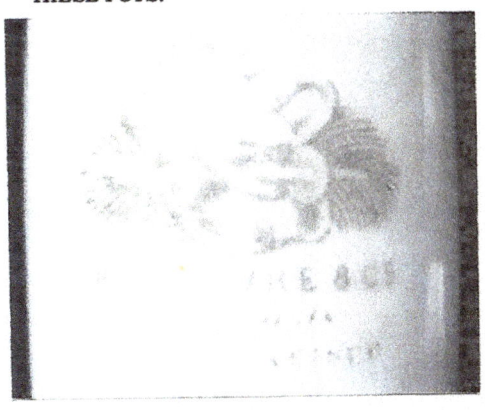

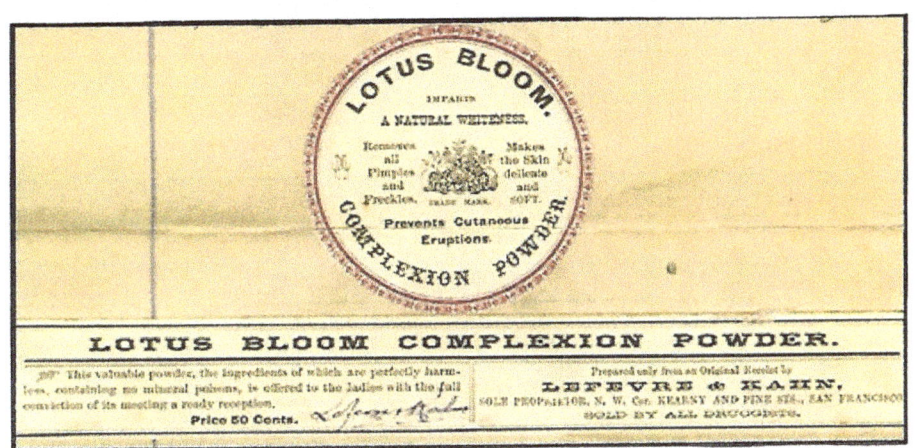

127

Top: SAPONACEOUS TOOTH POWDER / B.B. THAYER & CO. / APOTHECARIES / 121 MONTGOMERY STREET / SAN FRANCISCO / CALIFORNIA

ROUND CERAMIC LID, 3 ½" ACROSS
EX. RARE, $550.00- 1996

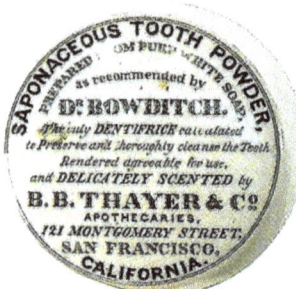

Side: B.B. THAYER & CO. / APOTHECARIES / SAN FRANCISCO / CAL.

ROUND CERAMIC POTS
Note: THESE COME in MANY DIFFERENT SIZES and LETTERING VARIENTS. THERE ARE JUST A FEW SHOWN HERE. ALL ARE RARE WITH THE LARGER ONES BEING THE RAREST.

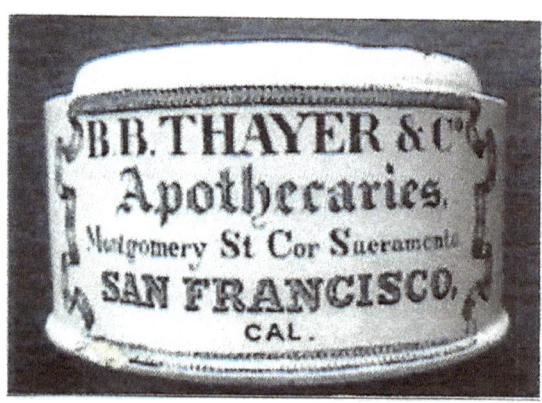

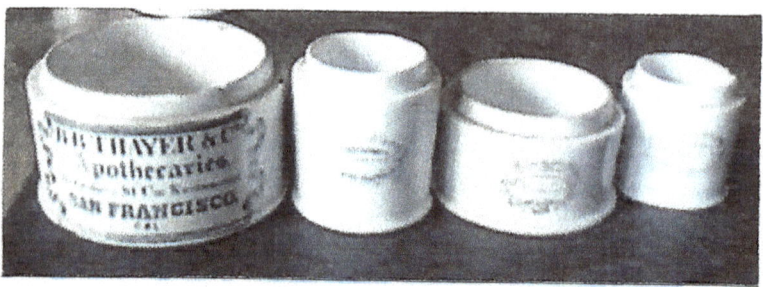

Top: H.P. WAKELEE DRUGGIST / BURDELL'S / TOOTH / POWDER / SAN FRANCISCO

ROUND, CERAMIC LID, 3" ACROSS
SCARCE, $325.00- 2020

Top: H.P. WAKELEE DRUGGIST / URSINA / SAN FRANCISCO

ROUND, CERAMIC LID, 3" ACROSS
EX. RARE, $2400.00- 2017
$600.00- 2020 (crack)

Top: H.P. WAKELEE DRUGGIST / ODONTO / SAN FRANCISCO

ROUND, CERAMIC LID, 3 ¼" ACROSS
EX. RARE, $2000.00- 2017
$750.00- 2020 (chip)

Top: H.P. WAKELEE DRUGGIST / COLD / CREAM / SAN FRANCISCO

ROUND, CERAMIC LID, 3" ACROSS
SCARCE, $275.00- 2002
$300.00- 2020 (repaired)
Note: AD CIRCA 1867

Top: **H.P. WAKELEE DRUGGIST / PHILICOME / SAN FRANCISCO**

ROUND, CERAMIC LID, 3" ACROSS
EX. RARE, $1000.00- 2017 (chips)
$650.00- 2020 (chip)

Top: **H.P. WAKELEE DRUGGIST / GENUINE / BEARS GREASE / SAN FRANCISCO**

ROUND, CERAMIC LID, 3" ACROSS
EX. RARE, $2600.00- 2017

Front: **CARL ZELLE / APOTHECARY / 328 PACIFIC STREET**

ROUND, CERAMIC POT, 2" TALL
EX. RARE
Locale: SAN FRANCISCO

Front: **BURDELL'S / ORIENTAL TOOTH POWDER / PREPARED BY / H.P. WAKELEE / DRUGGIST MONTGOMERY ST. / SAN FRANCISCO / CAL.**

ROUND, CERAMIC LID, 3" ACROSS
EX. RARE, $2000.00- 2020

Front: **DR. BOUTHMAR'S CELEBRATED / AROMATIC TOOTH PASTE / PREPARED ONLY BY H.W. SCHMIDT & BRO / SAN FRANCISCO**

ROUND, CERAMIC LID, 3" ACROSS
EX. RARE

Front: **V. CREVALLIAR / PHARMACIEN / 207 CLAY ST. / SAN FRANCISCO**

ROUND CERAMIC POT, 2 ½" TALL
RARE

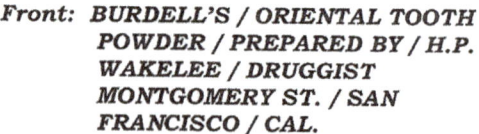

SARSAPARILLA TYPES

Front: ABRAMS & CARROLL / SOLE AGENTS / S.F.
Side: COMPOND EXTRACT
Side: SARSAPARILLA

   RECT., SMOOTH BASE, 9 ½"
   APPLIED and TOOLED TOP
   AQUA
   SCARCE with a TOOLED TOP
   RARE with an APPLIED TOP

Front: ABRAMS & CARROLL / SOLE AGENTS / S.F.
Side: COMPOND EXTRACT
Side: SARSAPARILLA
Re: HONDURAS CO'S

   RECT., SMOOTH BASE, 9 ½"
   APPLIED TOP
   AQUA, $150.00- 2017
   RARE

Front: DR. IRA BAKER'S / HONDURAS /
       SARSAPARILLA

   RECT., SMOOTH BASE, 10 ½"
   TOOLED TOP
   AQUA, $160.00- 2017
   SCARCE
   CIRCA: 1899

Front: BIXBY'S SARSAPARILLA / BIXBY'S
       DRUG STORE / SANTA CRUZ, CAL.

   RECT., SMOOTH BASE, 8 ¾"
   TOOLED TOP
   AQUA
   RARE

Front: J. CALIGARIS / COMPOUND EXTRACT /
       SARSAPARILL / SAN FRANCISCO, CAL.

   RECT., SMOOTH BASE, 8 ¾"
   TOOLED TOP
   AQUA, $120.00- 1997
   RARE

Front: CRANE & BRIGHAM / WHOLESALE
       DRUGGISTS / SAN FRANCISCO
Side: DR. LAMEROUX'S
Side: SARSAPARILLA

   RECT., SMOOTH BASE, 9" and 6 ¾"
   APPLIED TOP
   AQUA
   EX. RARE

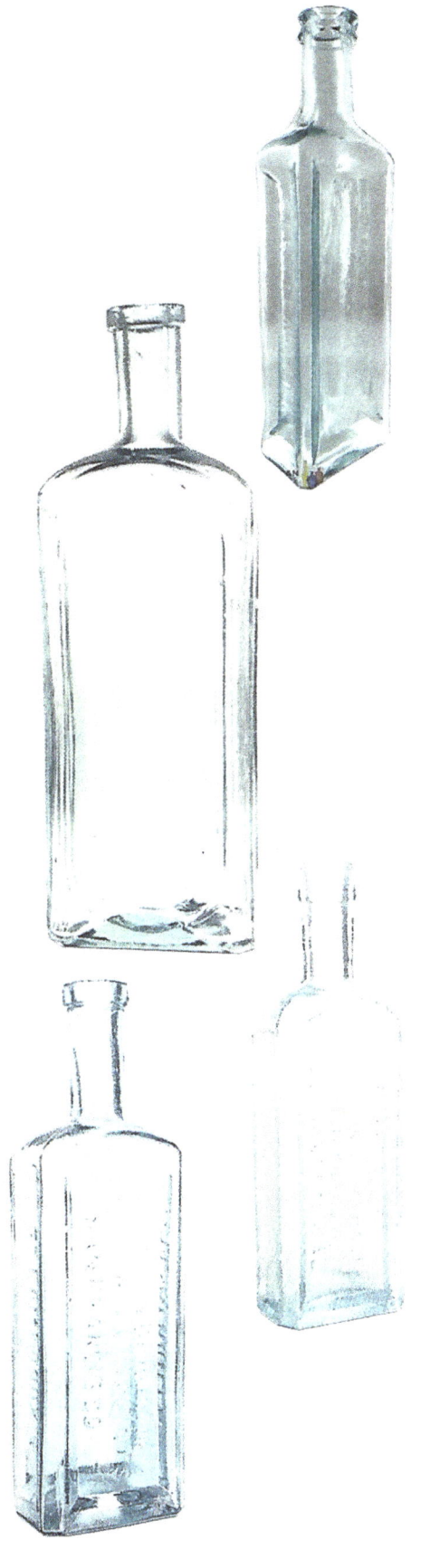

Front: **CROWELL, CRANE & BRIGHAM**
Side: **YELLOW DOCK**
Side: **SARSAPARILLA**

    RECT., OPEN PONTIL & SMOOTH BASE
    APPLIED TOP
    CLEAR FLINT GLASS
    AQUA, S.B., $600.00- 2017 (chip)
    AQUA, O.P., $3000.00- 2011
    Note: ONE of the WEST'S FIRST EMBOSSED
    MEDICINE TYPE BOTTLES. AD AT LOWER
    RIGHT FROM THE 1856 S.F. DIRECTORY.
    THE BONE HANDLE TOOTH BRUSH is an
    EX. RARE CROWELL, CRANE & BRIGHAM
    GO – WITH.

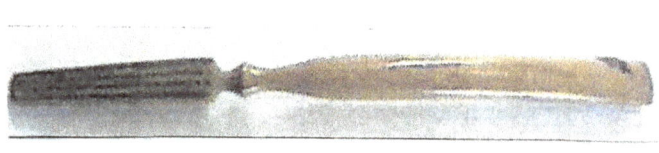

Front: **DR. COOPER'S / SARSAPARILLA / WOODWARD, CLARK & CO. / PORTLAND, ORE.**

    RECT., SMOOTH BASE, 10"
    TOOLED TOP
    AQUA, $70.00- 2006
    RARE

Front: **FRY'S SARSAPARILLA / SALEM, OREGON**

    RECT., SMOOTH BASE, 9 ½"
    TOOLED TOP
    AQUA
    RARE

Front: **HALL'S / SARSAPARILLA**
Side: **J.R. GATES & CO.**
Side: **PROPRIETORS, S.F.**

    RECT., SMOOTH BASE, 9 ½"
    APPLIED and TOOLED TOP
    AQUA, $70.00- 2006
    COMMON

Front: HALL'S / SARSAPARILLA
Side: SHEPARDSON & GATES
Side: PROPRIETORS, S.F.

    RECT., SMOOTH BASE, 9 ½"
    APPLIED and TOOLED TOP
    AQUA, A.T., $180.00- 1999
    EX. RARE in LIME GREEN
    SCARCE in AQUA

Front: DR. HENRY'S / SARSAPARILLA

    RECT, SMOOTH BASE, 9 ¼"
    APPLIED TOP
    AQUA, $100.00- 2017
    SCARCE
    Note: AT RIGHT is a PARTIAL LABEL
    FOR a DR. HENRY'S. REDINGTON
    & CO. WAS THE AGENT.

Front: THE / EDWIN W. JOY CO. /
       SAN FRANCISCO
Side: JOY'S
Side: SARSAPARILLA

    RECT., SMOOTH BASE, 8 ¾"
    TOOLED TOP
    AQUA, $50.00- 2019
    COMMON in AQUA
    RARE in LT. LIME GREEN

Front: JOY'S / VEGETABLE /
       SARSAPARILLA
Side: THE EDWIN JOY CO.
Side: SAN FRANCISCO, CAL.

    RECT., SMOOTH BASE, 8 ¾"
    TOOLED TOP
    AQUA
    RARE
    Note: BELOW is ONE of the MANY
    TRADE CARDS PUT OUT by the
    EDWIN JOY CO. LABEL WAS
    TRADE MARKED in 1890

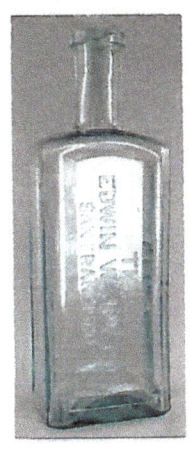
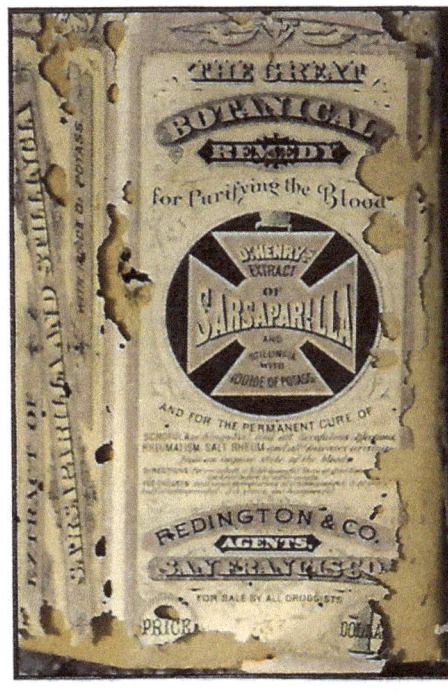

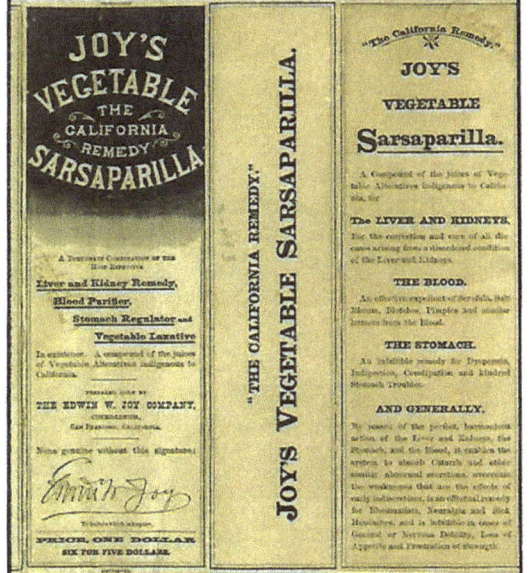

Front: CHAS. LANGLEY & CO. / SAN FRANCISCO
Side: COMPOUND EXTRACT
Side: SARSAPARILLA

RECT., SMOOTH BASE, 9 ½"
APPLIED and TOOLED TOP
AQUA, T.T., $110.00- 2017
SCARCE
Note: HAS WESTERN CURVED R's

Side: LANGLEY'S
Front: COMPOUND / SARSAPARIILA
Side: SAN FRANCISCO

RECT., IRON PONTIL and SMOOTH BASE
APPLIED TOP, 10 ½" x 3 ¾" x 2 ¼"
GREENISH AQUA, S.B., $2200.00- 2017
GREEN
EX. RARE in ALL VARIENTS, COLORS.

Front: **LEVING'S & CO.**
Side: **SARSAPARILLA / AND / ROSE WILLOW**

SQUARE, SMOOTH BASE, 7 ¾"
APPLIED and TOOLED TOP
LT. AQUA, T.T., $400.00- 2006
DEEP AQUA, A.T., $1500.00- 2017
EX. RARE
Note: TOOLED TOP EXAMPLES APPEAR
TO BE EASTERN BLOWN.

Side: **J.J. MACK & CO.**
Front: **INDIAN / SARSAPARILLA**
Side: **SAN FRANCISCO, CAL.**
Re: motif of INDIAN WARRIOR

RECT., SMOOTH BASE, 9"
TOOLED TOP
AQUA, DCT, $300.00- 2019
RARE
Note: THESE HAVE 2 TYPES of
TOOLED TOPS and THE
WESTERN CURVED R's.

Front: **MEYER'S SARSAPARILLA / MANF'D
BY / GIANT MEDICINE CO. /
HELENA, MONT.**

RECT., SMOOTH BASE, 9 ¼"
TOOLED TOP
AQUA
EX. RARE

Front: **PORTER'S SARSAPARILLA /
PREPARED BY / HIRAM
POND / HOLLISTER, CAL.**

RECT., SMOOTH BASE, 8 ¼"
TOOLED TOP
AQUA
RARE

Front: **DR. SIGNORETT'S COMP. EXT. /
SARSAPARILLA / A.B. STEWART
SEATTLE**

RECT., SMOOTH BASE, 8 ½"
TOOLED TOP
AQUA
EX. RARE
Note: AD CIRCA 1886

Signoretts Compound Extract of Sarsaparilla
—THE—
Great Blood Purifier.
—FOR SALE BY—
A. B. STEWART, Druggist,
615 - - - - Front Street.

Front: DR. SIGNORETTS COMP EXT. / SARSAPARILLA /
STEWART & HOLMES DRUG CO. SEATTLE

RECT., SMOOTH BASE, 8 ½"
TOOLED TOP
AQUA
EX. RARE
CIRCA: 1889-1900

Front: DR. SIGNORETT'S * * * /
SARSAPARILLA / A.B.
STEWART & BRO. /
TACOMA, WASH.

RECT., SMOOTH BASE, 8 ½"
TOOLED TOP
AQUA
EX. RARE
Note: AD CIRCA 1887

DR. SIGNORETT'S 3 STAR SARSAPARILLA!
The Great Blood Purifier,

Cures Scrofula and all Scrofulous Taints, Eruptions of the Skin, Pimples, Boils, Salt Rheum, Ring Worm, Catarrh, and all Diseases arising from Impurity of the Blood. It enriches the Complexion and infuses New Life, health and vigor throughout the whole system. For sale by A. B. STEWART.

Front: WHITNEY'S / SARSAPARILLA /
PUT UP BY / MILLER & WHITNEY /
HEALDSBURG, CALA.

RECT., SMOOTH BASE, 9 ½"
TOOLED TOP
AQUA
Varient: WHITNEY & KRUSE
Varient: WHITNEY'S PHARMACY
ALL VARIENTS are EX. RARE

EARLY APOTHECARY and DRUG STORE TYPES

Front: J.A. BAUER / S.F. CAL.

RECT., SMOOTH BASE, 8 ½"
APPLIED TOP
AQUA
GREEN
EX. RARE
Note: AD BELOW is CIRCA 1867

J. A. BAUER,
DRUG STORE,
Chemical Laboratory and Assay Office,
644 WASHINGTON STREET, SAN FRANCISCO, CAL.
CAREFUL ANALYSES MADE OF
Ores, Minerals, Waters, Oils, Liquors, Products of Art, &c.
PHARMACEUTICAL PREPARATIONS MADE TO ORDER.
Opinions given on Chemical Questions and Geology.
Nitrate of Silver in Crystals or fused, and Chloride of Gold and Sodium for sale.

Front: J. DOHERTY / BOSTON / DRUG STORE / SACRAMENTO

ROUND, SMOOTH BASE, VARIOUS SIZES
FLAIR TOP
AQUA
CLEAR, 5 ½", $70.00- 2011
COMMON
Note: THE LARGER SIZES ARE EMBOSSED in THREE LINES INSTEAD of FOUR.
AD is CIRCA 1863-1864.

BOSTON DRUG STORE.
J. DOHERTY,
IMPORTER, WHOLESALE AND RETAIL DEALER IN
Drugs, Chemicals, Patent Medicines, Etc.
CONSTANTLY ON HAND A LARGE ASSORTMENT OF
French, English and German Perfumery, Toilet Goods, Etc., Etc.
No. 53 J Street, between Second and Third Sts.
SACRAMENTO.

Front: J.B. CUNNINGWORTH / APOTHECARY / SAN FRANCISCO

ROUND, SMOOTH BASE, 5"
APPLIED TOP
AQUA, $900.00- 2006
EX. RARE

Front: **H. BOWMAN / DRUGGIST**
Side: **262 J. STREET**
Side: **SACRAMENTO**

RECT., SMOOTH BASE, 7 ¼"
APPLIED TOP
AQUA, $90.00- 2017
Note: THIS BOTTLE COULD HAVE HELD
ANY OF THE PRODUCTS SHOWN
HERE. HORSE MEDICINE AD is CIRCA
1870's. LINIMENT LABEL WAS TRADE
MARKED in 1872 AND THE RICHARD'S
LABEL WAS TRADE MARKED in 1866.

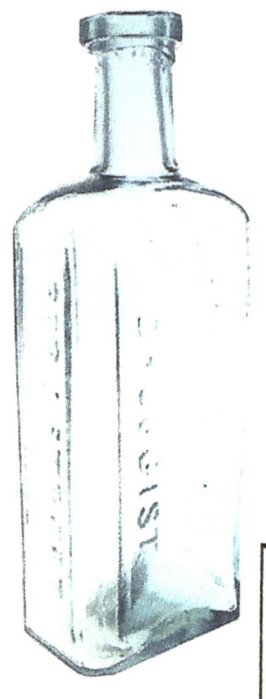
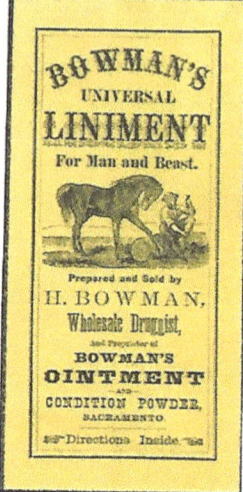
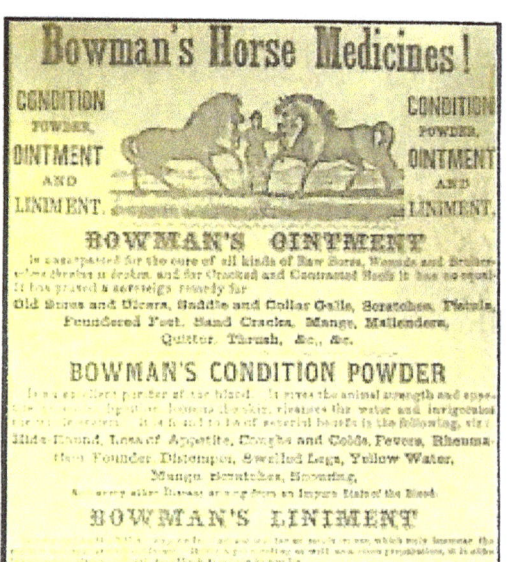
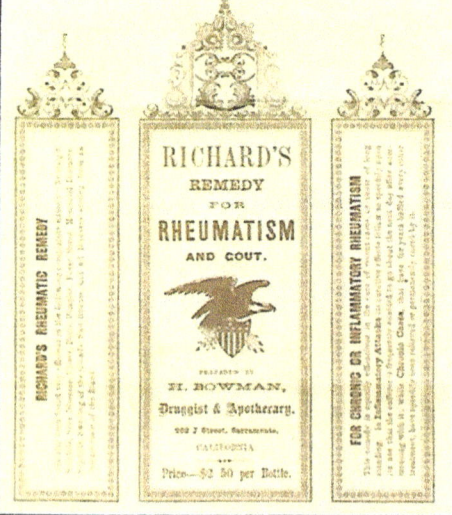

Front: **R.E. GOGINGS / DRUGGIST**
Side: **262 J STREET**
Side: **SACRAMENTO**

RECT., SMOOTH BASE, 7 ½"
TOOLED TOP
AQUA
SCARCE
Note: LABEL AT RIGHT WAS
TRADE MARKED in 1890.
EITHER OF THESE GOGINGS
BOTTLES COULD HAVE HELD
THIS PRODUCT.

Front: **R.E. GOGINGS**
Side: **262 J STREET**
Side: **SACRAMENTO**

RECT., SMOOTH BASE, 5 ¾"
APPLIED and FLAIRED TOP
AQUA, COBALT
AMBER, $180.00- 2004
AQUA and AMBER are RARE
COBALT is EX. RARE

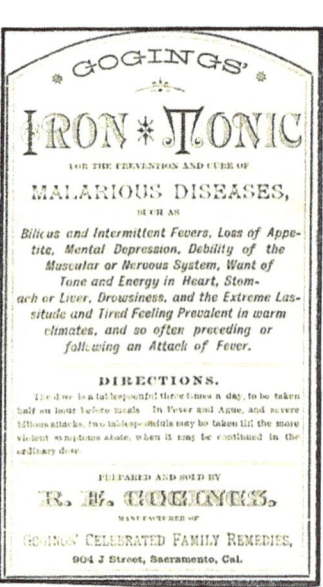

Front: **H.A. ELLIOTT / PHARMACIST / IDAHO SPRINGS, COLO.**

    RECT., SMOOTH BASE, 6 ¾"
    APPLIED TOP
    AQUA
    RARE

Front: **R.R. HAY / DRUGGIST / S.F.**

    ROUND, SMOOTH BASE
    APPLIED TOP, 4 ½"
    AQUA
    RARE

Front: **KEATING & BABB / SAN JOSE**

    RECT., SMOOTH BASE, 5 ½" and 6 ¼"
    TOOLED TOP
    COBALT, $6 ¼", $1200.00- 2013
    EX. RARE

Front: **H.T. KELLY / MARYSVILLE**

    OVAL, OPEN PONTIL, 7 ½"
    APPLIED TOP
    AQUA, $1200.00- 2017
    EX. RARE
    Varient: EMBOSSING is VERTICAL

Front: **C.P. POLLARD / DRUGGIST / MAYSVILLE**

    OVAL, OPEN PONTIL, 7 ½"
    APPLIED TOP
    AQUA, $400.00- 1999
    RARE
    Note: "MARYSVILLE" is MISSPELLED, AD is CIRCA 1861.

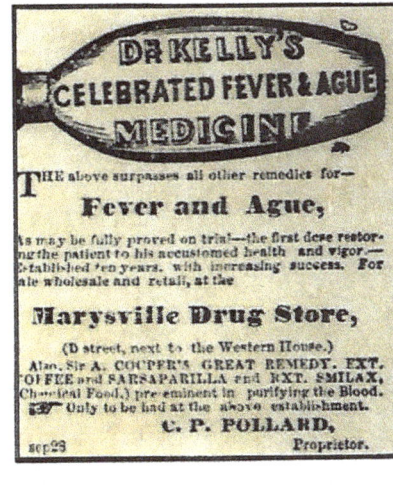

Front: **WM. H. KEITH & CO. / SAN FRANCISCO**

    ROUND, SMOOTH BASE, VARIOUS SIZES
    FLAIR TOP
    CLEAR FLINT GLASS
    RARE
    Note: ANY of the KEITH BOTTLES COULD
           HAVE HELD THE PRODUCT BELOW
           IN THE CIRCA 1860's AD.

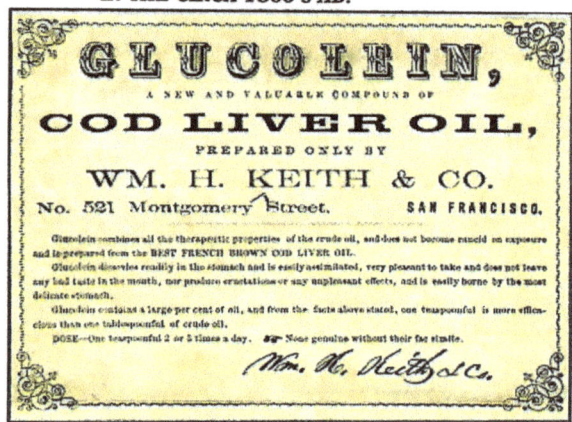

Front: **WM. H. KEITH & CO. / SAN FRANCISCO**

    OVAL, SMOOTH BASE, 5 ¾"
    APPLIED TOP
    AQUA
    EX. RARE

Front: **WM. H. KEITH & CO. / APOTHECARIES / SAN FRANCISCO**

    OVAL, SMOOTH BASE, 7" and 8 ½"
    APPLIED TOP
    AQUA
    EX. RARE
    Varient: HAS SMALLER EMBOSSING FONT.
       CLEAR FLINT GLASS, 8" and 8 ½"
       EX. RARE

Front: **B. LEFEVRE & CO. / APOTHECARIES / SAN FRANCSICO**

    ROUND, OPEN PONTIL, VARIOUS SIZES
    FLAIR TOP
    CLEAR FLINT GLASS
    EX. RARE

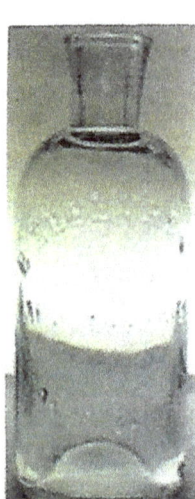

Front: E. PETIBEAU & CO. / DRUGGISTS /
       motif of cherub flying over mortar & pestle /
       9th & HOWARD STS. / S.F.

   RECT., SMOOTH BASE, 7"
   TOOLED TOP
   CLEAR
   EX. RARE

Front: W.B. PIXLEY / APOTHECARY /
       STOCKTON (in round plate)

   ROUND, SMOOTH BASE, VARIOUS SIZES
   TOOLED TOP
   CLEAR
   SCARCE

Front: monogram / W.B. PIXLEY / DRUGGIST /
       STOCKTON, CAL.

   RECT., SMOOTH BASE, 5 ½"
   TOOLED TOP
   AMBER
   RARE
   Note: EARLY TRADE CARD BELOW.

Front: H. McCOMAS / STOCKTON

   BONE HANDLE TOOTH BRUSH, 6 ¼"
   EX. RARE GO-WITH

Front: E.F. SPENCE / NEVADA

   ROUND, SMOOTH BASE, 4 ¾"
   FLAIR TOP
   CLEAR FLINT GLASS
   EX. RARE
   CIRCA: 1860's
   Locale: NEVADA CITY, CAL.

Front: J.B. SCOTT / PHARMACIST / SALINAS, CAL.

    RECT., SMOOTH BASE, 9"
    TOOLED TOP
    AQUA, $180.00- 2017
    RARE

Front: monogram / THE UNIVERSITY / BOOK & DRUG STORE / BOULDER, COLO.

    SQUARE, SMOOTH BASE, 8"
    TOOLED TOP
    AMBER
    RARE

Front: H.P. WAKELEE / DRUGGIST / SAN FRANCISCO

    ROUND, SMOOTH BASE, VARIOUS SIZES
    FLAIR TOP
    CLEAR FLINT GLASS
    RARE

Front: H.P. WAKELEE / DRUGGIST / SAN FRANCISCO

    OVAL, SMOOTH BASE, 3 ½"
    ROLLED LIP
    CLEAR
    EX. RARE

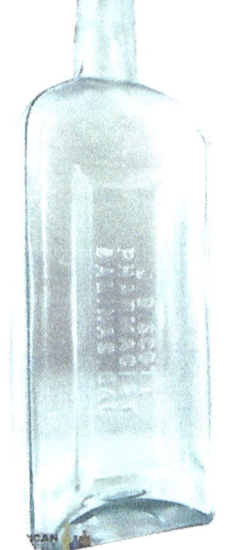

Front: H.P. WAKELEE & CO. / monogram / SAN FRANCISCO

    RECT., SMOOTH BASE, 5 ½"
    TOOLED TOP
    CLEAR
    SCARCE

Front: W.H. WOOD / APOTHECARY / SAN FRANCISCO, / CAL.

    ROUND, SMOOTH BASE, 3 ¾"
    TOOLED TOP
    CLEAR
    RARE

THE FOLLOWING FEW PAGES CONTAIN A SELECTION OF ADS, TRADE MARK LABELS, BILLHEADS, AND A FEW PRODUCT TRADE CARDS. ALL OF THESE ARE FROM CALIFORNIA AND MOST DO NOT HAVE AN EMBOSSED BOTTLE TO GO WITH THE TRADE MARK OR AD.

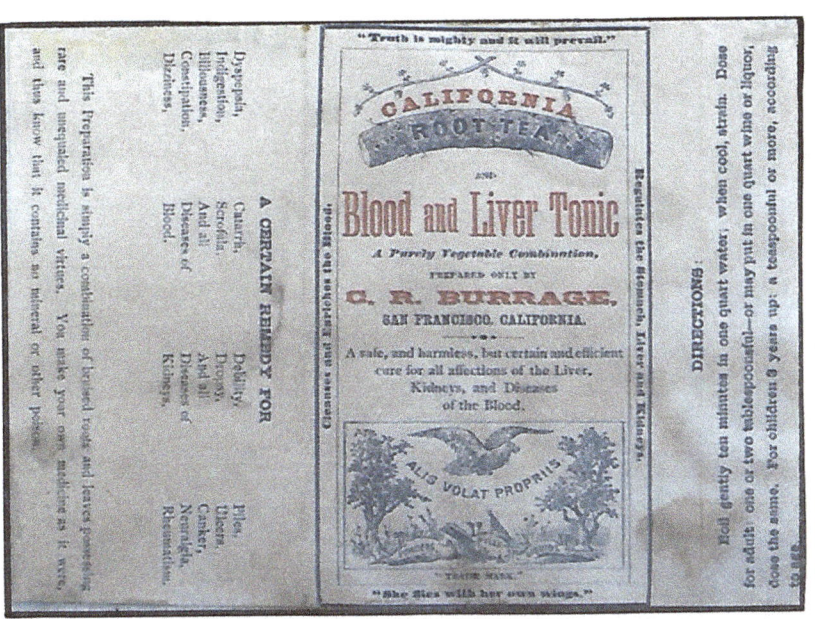

CALIFORNIA ROOT TEA BLOOD & LIVER TONIC LABEL
TRADE MARKED in 1879 by C.R. BURRAGE, S.F.

SIBERIAN BALSAM LABEL
TRADE MARKED in 1882
by W.K. DIETRICH, S.F.

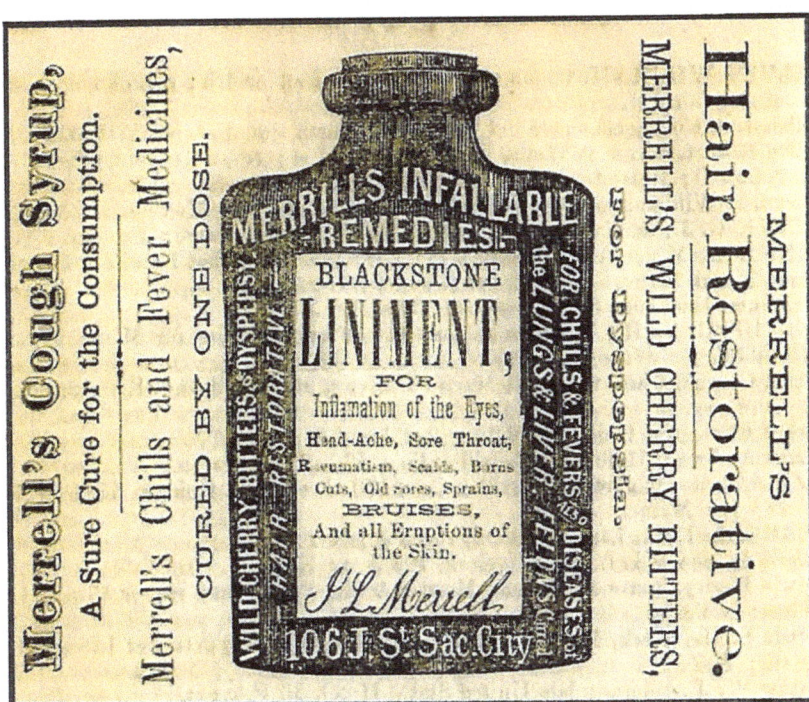

MERRILL'S INFALLABLE REMEDIES, 106 J ST.
SACRAMENTO. AD CIRCA 1866

CIRCASSIAN TONIC LABEL
TRADE MARKED in 1873
by CASPAR LANDIS, S.F.

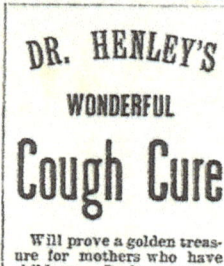

DR. HENLEY'S COUGH CURE LABEL, FRONT and BACK
TRADE MARKED in 1885 by WILLIAM HENLEY of
ALAMEDA. REDINGTON & CO. S.F. WERE THE AGENTS

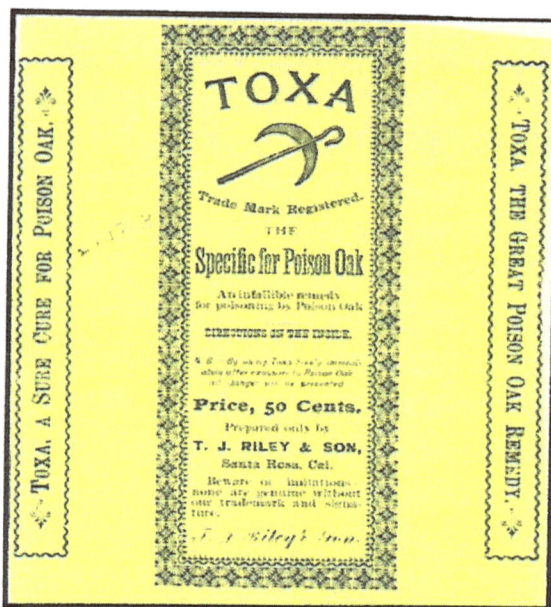

TOXA POISON OAK SPECIFIC LABEL. TRADE
MARKED in 1889 by T.J. RILEY & SONS
SANTA ROSA

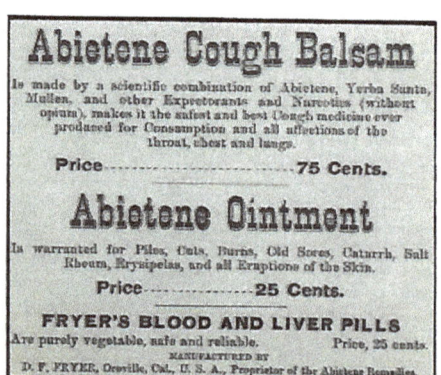

ABIETINE COUGH BALSAM AD.
CIRCA 1886, FROM OROVILLE, CA.

FLINT'S ORIENTAL SACHET POWDER LABEL.
TRADE MARKED in 1889 by GEORGE B. FLINT
of FLINT'S PHARMACY, OAKLAND CA.

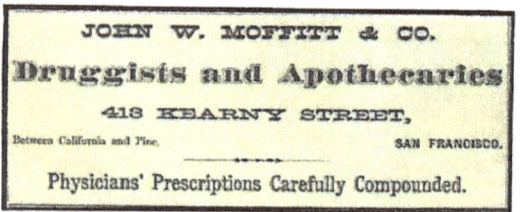

BROOKLYN DRUG STORE AD, CIRCA 1871-72
BROOKLYN IS NOW PART of OAKLAND, CA.

JOHN W. MOFFIT & CO. APOTHECARIES AD.
CIRCA 1872. THIS IS THE MOFFIT PARTNER
of MERTEN & MOFFIT FAME.

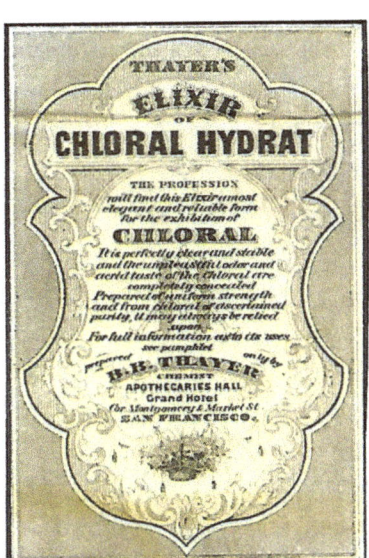

THAYER'S ELIXIR OF CHLORAL HYDRAT
LABEL TRADE MARKED in 1870 by
B.B. THAYER, S.F.

INDIAN CHARM OIL LINIMENT. LABEL TRADE
MARKED in 1884 by WILLIAM RICHE, S.F.

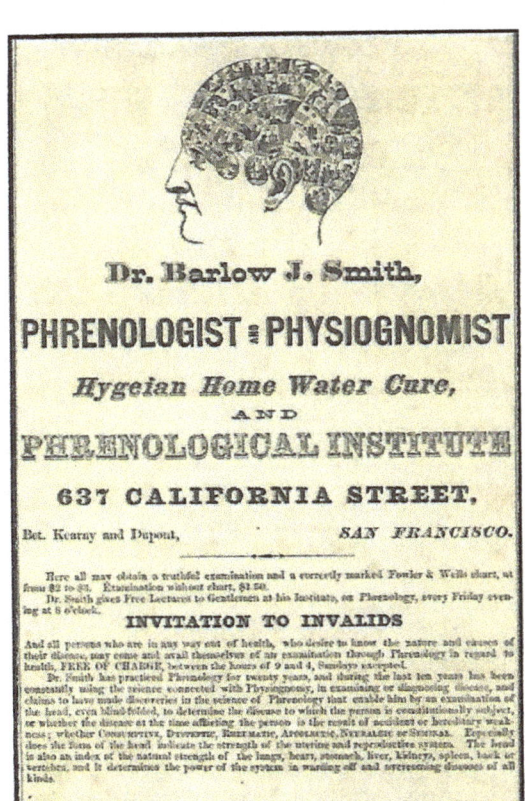

BARLOW J. SMITH PHRENOLOGICAL INSTITUTE.
AD CIRCA 1872 in SAN FRANCISCO.

DR. G.A. BARTH'S CALIFORNIA CREAM LINIMENT
LABEL TRADE MARKED in 1889 by G.A. BARTH,
SAN JOSE. CA. AGENTS WERE J.J. MACK &
LANGLEY and MICHAELS in SAN FRANCISCO

LAMBERT'S HORSE LINIMENT LABEL. TRADE
MARKED in 1888 by EDWARD LAMBERT, NAPA

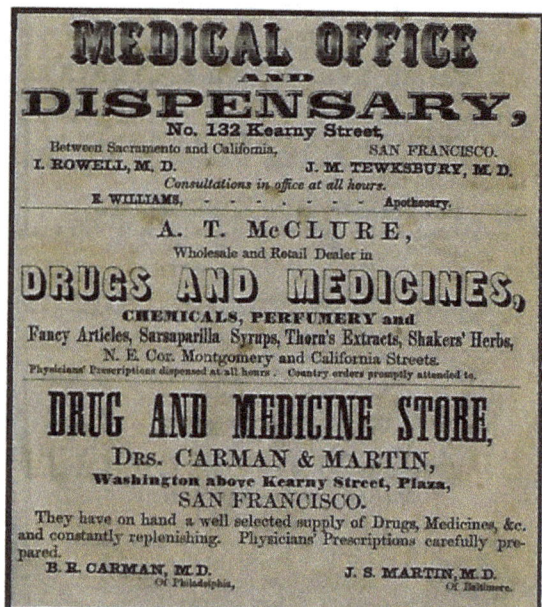

EARLY MEDICAL OFFICE and DISPENSARY
AD. CIRCA 1852-53 in SAN FRANCISCO

OLIVER'S HAIR KING LABEL. TRADE
MARKED in 1871 by G.A. OLIVER,
PACHECO, CA.

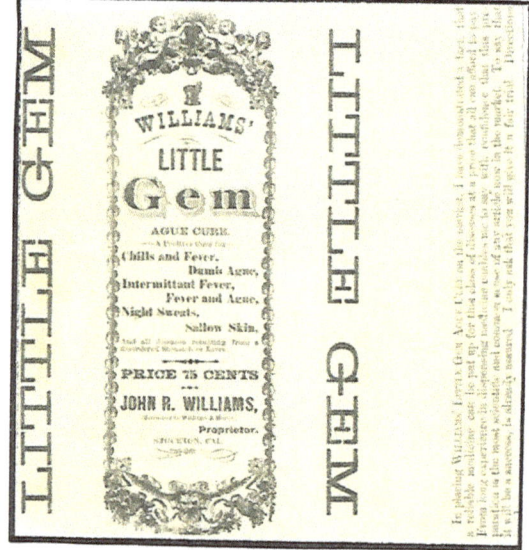

WILLIAMS LITTLE GEM AGUE CURE LABEL.
TRADE MARKED in 1880 by JOHN R.
WILLIAMS, STOCKTON, CA.

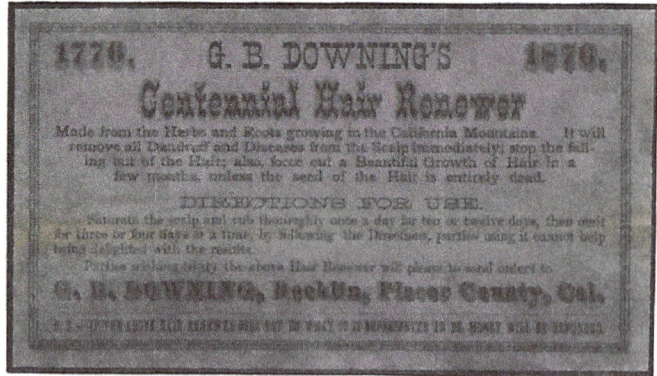

DOWNING'S CENTENNIAL HAIR RENEWER LABEL.
TRADE MARKED in 1878 by G.B. DOWNING, ROCKLIN CA.

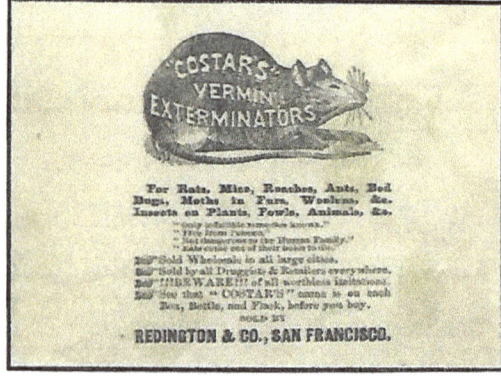

COSTAR'S VERMIN EXTERMINATOR AD. CIRCA
1878. REDINGTON & CO. S.F. AGENT

MODOC KIDNEY & LIVER CURE
LABEL. TRADE MARKED in 1888
by WM. J. HUSTED, MILLVILLE
SHASTA CO. CAL.

DR. MERRIMAN'S KALLIODONT
LABEL. TRADE MARKED in 1883
by A.F. MERRIMAN & SON
OAKLAND, CAL.

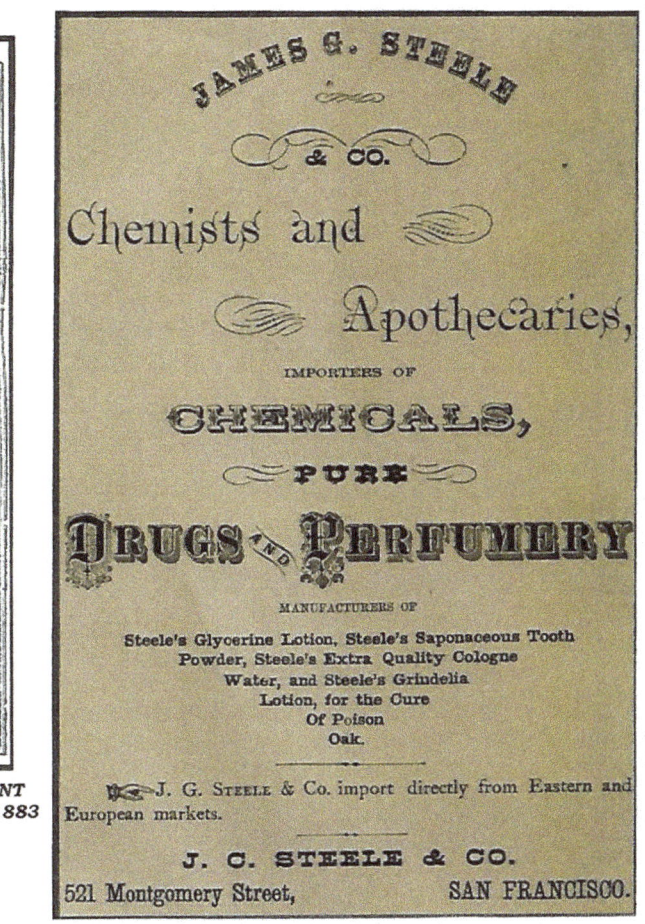

JAMES STEELE APOTHECARIES AD. CIRCA
1873, SAN FRANCISCO

NEEDHAM'S RED CLOVER TONIC
LABEL. TRADE MARKED in 1884
By W.C. NEEDHAM, SAN JOSE, CA.

LIGHTNING HAIR VIGOR
LABEL. TRADE MARKED
in 1889 by SAMUEL
LEWIS, GLEN ELLEN CA.

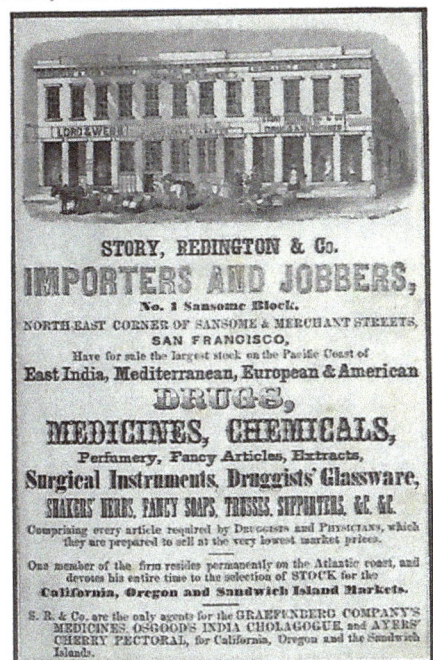

STORY & REDINGTON & CO. AD.
CIRCA 1854 SAN FRANCISCO

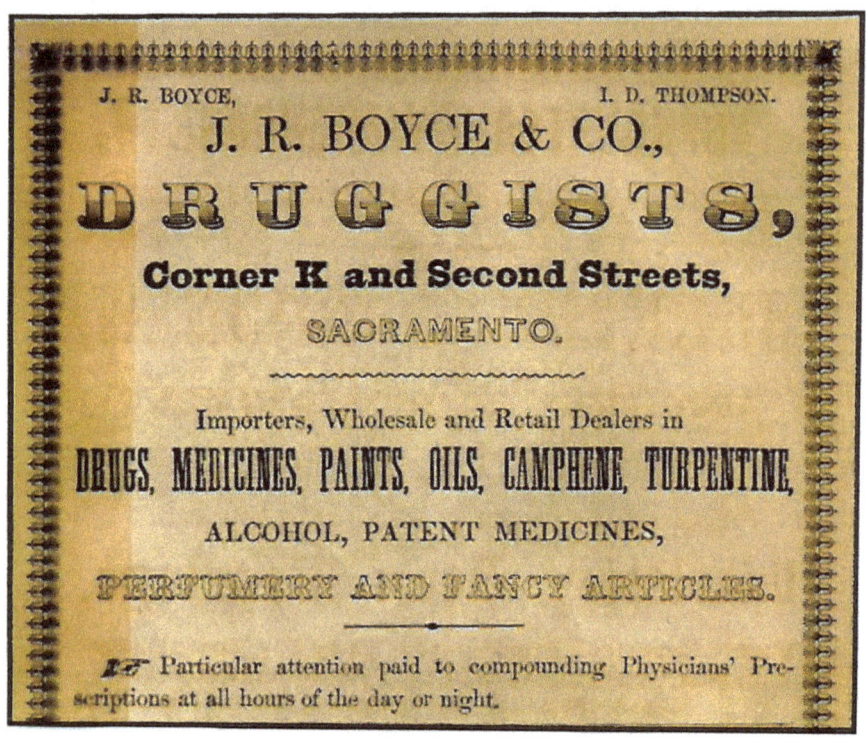

**J.R. BOYCE & CO. DRUGGISTS AD CIRCA 1856
SACRAMENTO**

**DR. THOS. HALL'S COUGH
MIXTURE AD. CIRCA 1878 S.F.**

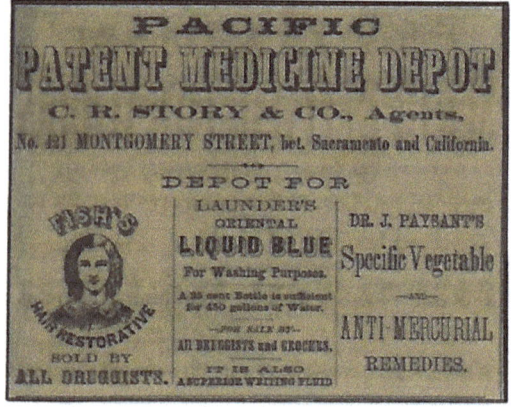

**PACIFIC PATENT MEDICINE DEPOT AD.
CIRCA 1861 in SAN FRANCISCO**

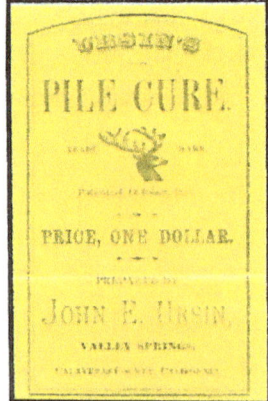

**URSIN'S PILE CURE LABEL
TRADE MARKED in 1885 by
JOHN URSIN, VALLEY SPRINGS,
CALAVERAS CO. CAL.**

**MacLENNAN'S CURE LABEL.
TRADE MARKED in 1885 by
JOHN MacLENNAN of S.F.**

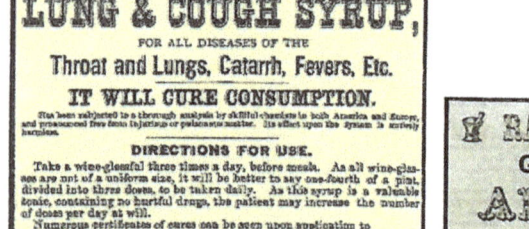

**HASSMER'S LUNG & COUGH CURE
S.F. AD. CIRCA 1880-81**

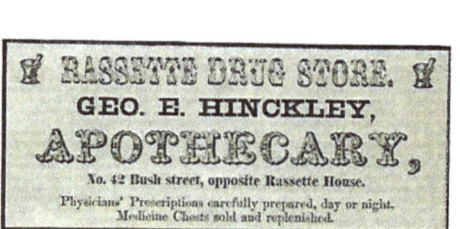

**HINCKLEY APOTHECARY S.F.
AD CIRCA 1856**

**HORSEMAN'S HOOF OINTMENT
LABEL. TRADE MARKED in 1871
HOMER WILLIAMS S.F.**

BESSEMER'S BOTANICAL SHAMPOO LABEL
TRADE MARKED in 1885 by H.L. BESSEMER S.F.

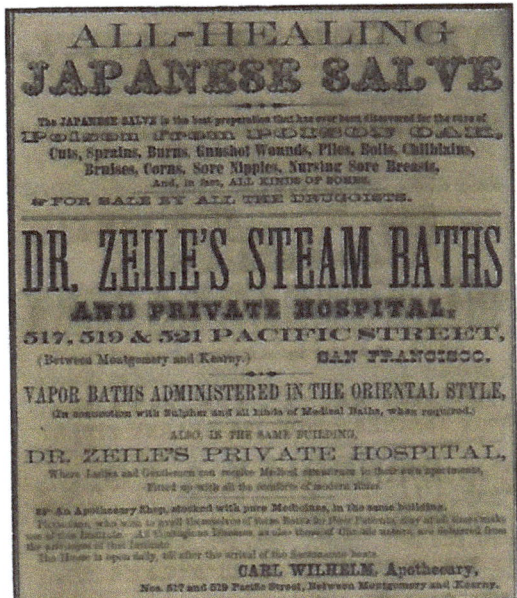

DR. ZEILE'S BATH with CARL WILHELM
APOTHEACARY AD. CIRCA 1861 in S.F.

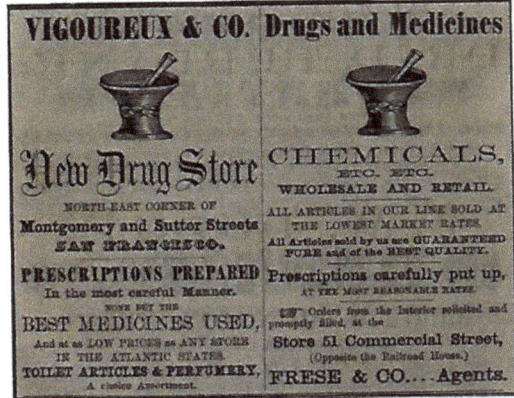

VIGOUREUX & CO. DRUS with E. FRESE
& CO. AGENT. CIRCA 1861 AD in S.F.

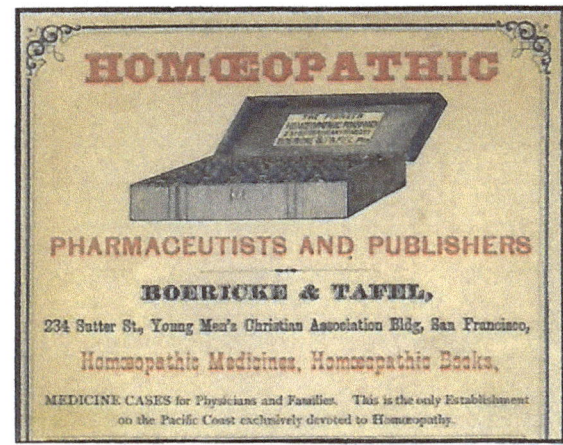

BOERICKE & TAFEL PHARMACISTS
S.F. AD CIRCA 1871.

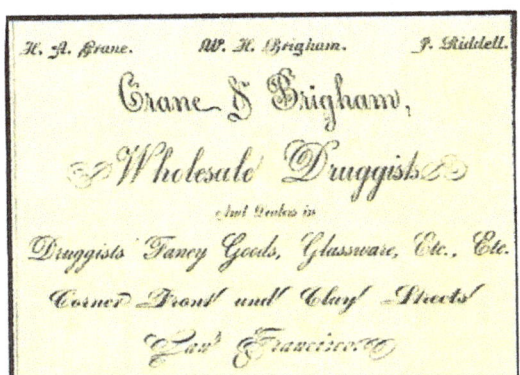

CRANE & BRIGHAM DRUGGISTS S.F.
AD CIRCA 1864

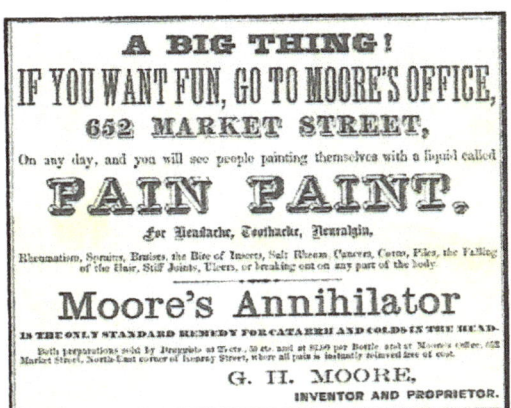

MOORE'S ANNIHILATOR PAIN PAINT
S.F. AD CIRCA 1860.

JAMES STEELE APOTHEACRIES S.F. AD
CIRCA 1876

LEMON EXTRACT LABEL
TRADE MARKED in 1896
by MERTEN MFG. S.F.

LIEBIG'S EUCALYPTUS TONIC
LABEL. TRADE MARKED in 1881
by COMMIUS & O. CONNER S.F.

PARADISE FOOT CURE LABEL. TRADE
MARKED in 1877 by WILLLIAM SCOLLAY S.F.

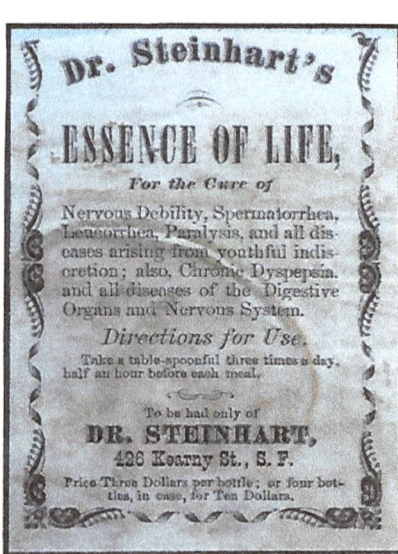

DR. STEINHART'S ESSENCE of LIFE
LABEL TRADE MARKED in 1877 by
PHILIP STEINHART S.F.

LEFFLER DRUGGIST STOCKTON TRADE CARD

MOTHER CARY'S SALVE. LABEL TRADE MARKED in 1882 by WILLIAM TYNDALE S.F.

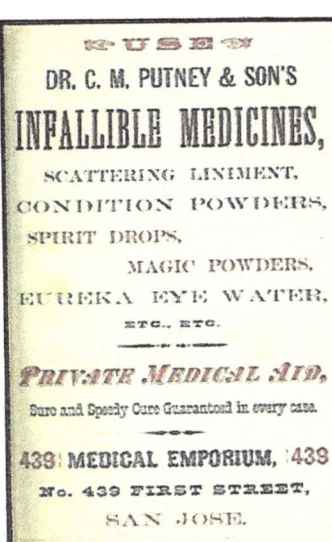

THAYER'S THEOLINE LABEL. TRADE MARKED in 1866 by B.B. THAYER S.F.

C.M. PUTNEY'S MEDICINES SAN JOSE. AD CIRCA 1871

SPIRIT PAIN RELIEF LABEL. TRADE MARKED in 1879 by WILLIAM COLLIER SACTO.

BARLOW J. SMITH WATER CURE S.F. AD CIRCA 1860

J.J. SPIEKER AGENTS FOR HOMER'S KIDNEY & LIVER CURE SACRAMENTO TRADE CARD

EARLY NEVADA APOTHECARY BOTTLES and ADVERTISMENTS

Front: A.M. COLE / APOTHECARY / VIRGINIA CITY, NEV.

    RECT., SMOOTH BASE, 5 ¾"
    TOOLED TOP
    AMBER, $1100.00- 2007
    EX. RARE

Front: A.M. COLE / VIRGINIA CITY

    RECT., SMOOTH BASE, 8 ½"
    APPLIED TOP
    BLUE AQUA, $950.00- 2007
    RARE

Front: A.M. COLE / DRUGGIST / VIRGINIA

    SQUARE, SMOOTH BASE, 8"
    FLAIR TOP
    AQUA
    EX. RARE
    Note: AD is CIRCA 1870's

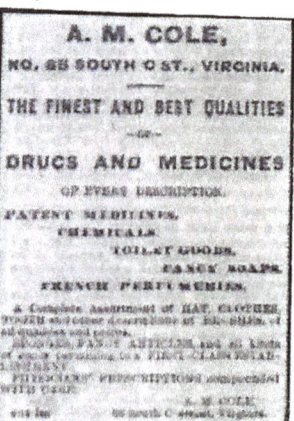

Front: J.B.B. LEFEVRE / DRUGGIST / VIRGINIA CITY, NEV.

    RECT., SMOOTH BASE, 8"
    APPLIED TOP
    AQUA, $325.00- 2002 (chip)
    Note: AD BELOW is CIRCA 1876

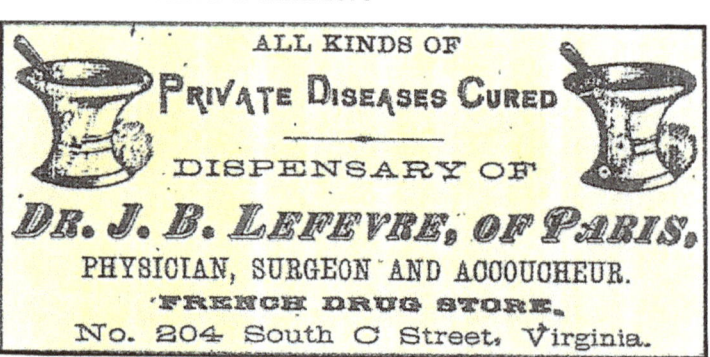

Front: C.C. THAXTER / DRUGGIST / mortar & pestle / CARSON

    SQUARE, SMOOTH BASE, 8"
    TOOLED TOP
    AQUA
    RARE

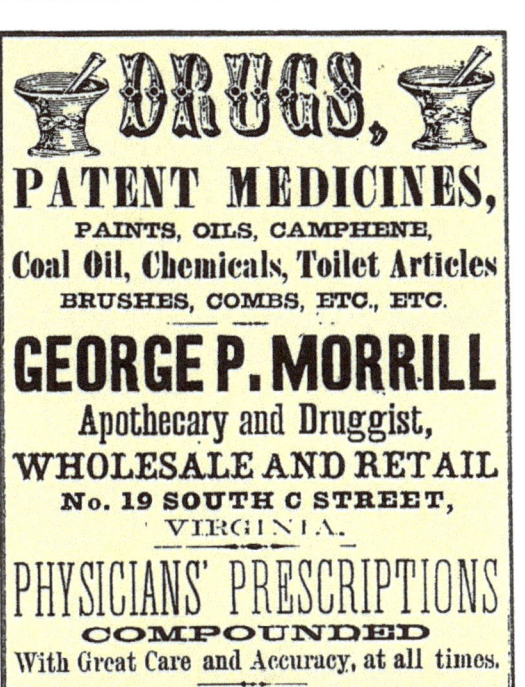

GEO. P. MORRILL VIRGINA AD CIRCA 1863

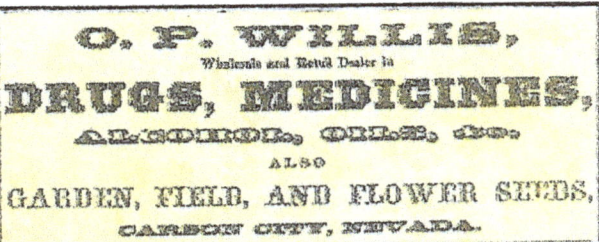

O.P. WILLIS CARSON CITY AD CIRCA 1867

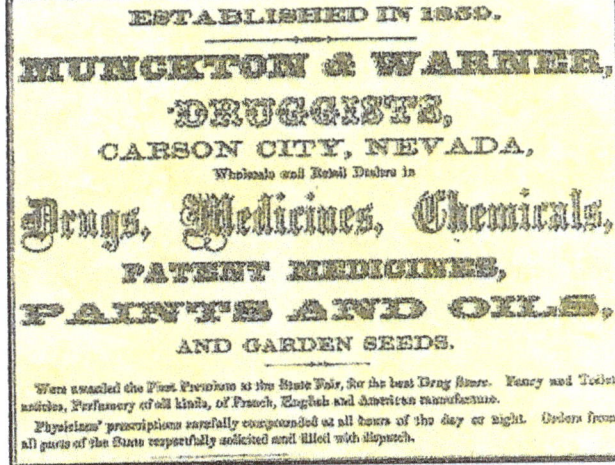

MUNCKTON & WARNER CARSON CITY AD CIRCA 1867

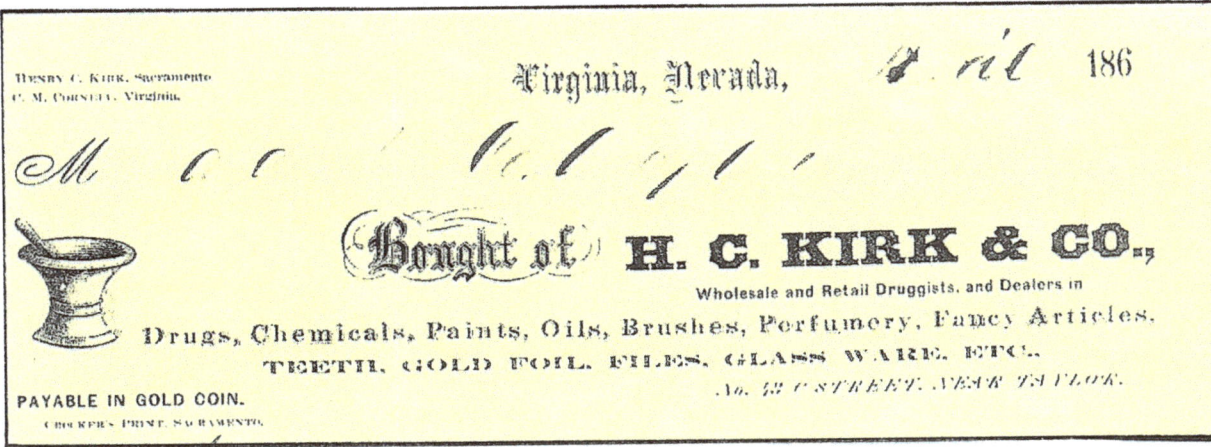

H.C. KIRK VIRGINIA NEVADA BILLHEAD CIRCA 1860's

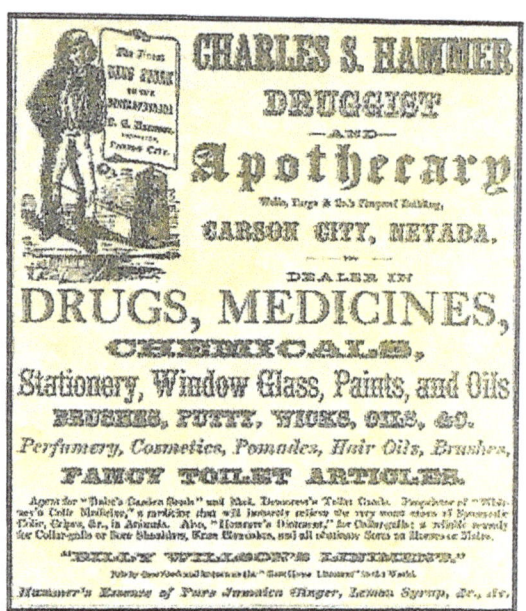

CHARLES HAMMER CARSON CITY AD CIRCA 1867

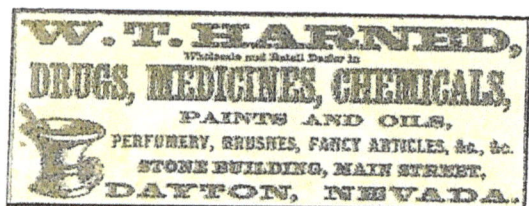

WILLIS & REED WASHOE CITY AD
CIRCA 1867

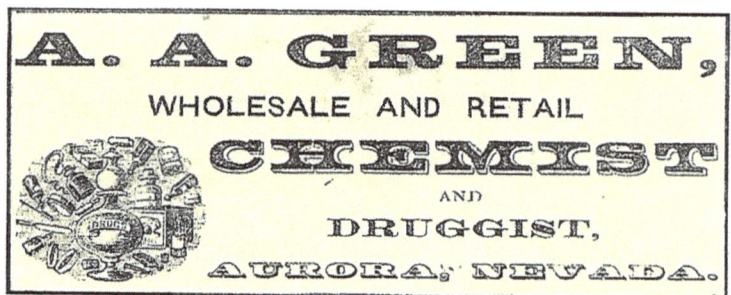

W.T. HARNED DAYTON NEVADA AD
CIRCA 1867

A.A. GREEN AURORA NEVADA AD CIRCA 1867

EARLY OREGON APOTHECARY BOTTLES and ADS

Front: motif of baby / WM. PFUNDER & CO. / DRUGGISTS / PORTLAND, OR.

    RECT., SMOOTH BASE, 5 ¾"
    TOOLED TOP
    TEAL GREEN, $400.00- 2006
    RARE

Front: motif of baby / WM. PFUNDER / DRUGGIST / PORTLAND, OR.

    RECT., SMOOTH BASE, 6 ¼"
    TOOLED TOP
    AMBER, $275.00- 2006
    RARE

Front: SMITH & DAVIS / PORTLAND OREGON

    SQUARE, SMOOTH BASE, 4 ¼"
    FLAIR TOP
    AQUA
    RARE
    CIRCA 1860's
    Note: SMITH & DAVIS AD BELOW is CIRCA 1867, THE T.A. DAVIS AD is CIRCA 1876.

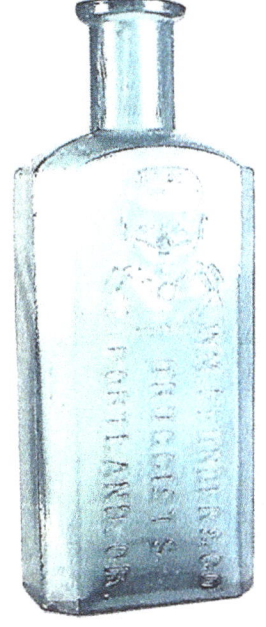

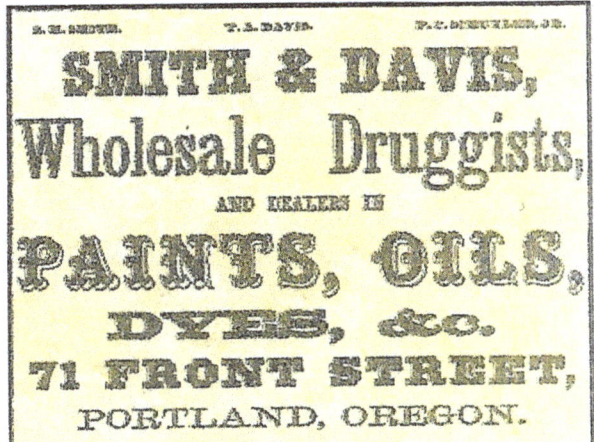
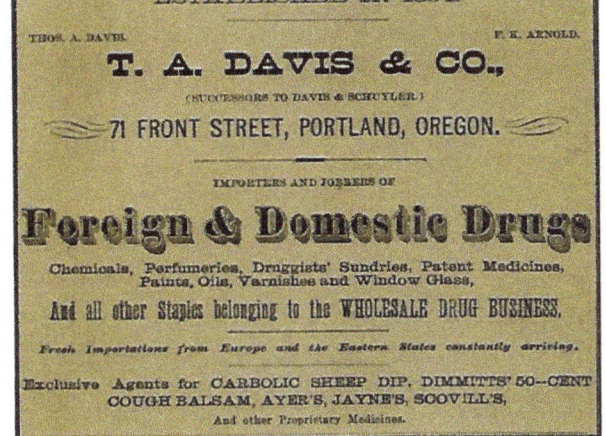

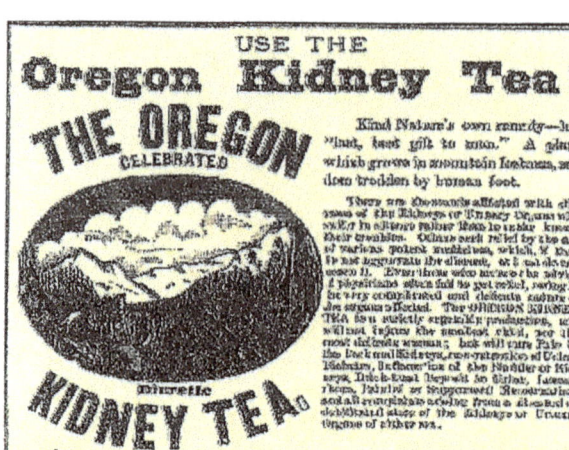

OREGON KIDNEY TEA AD CIRCA 1880-81

WEB FOOT TONIC AD CIRCA 1867

DR. MURRAY CORVALLIS ORE AD CIRCA 1867

BOTTLE INDEX

ABEL'S WHITE PINE BALSAM	65
ABIETINE MEDICAL CO, THE	70, 83
ABOLITION OIL	99, 109
ABRAMS & CARROLL	56, 131
ABRAMSON & BACON	1
ACME MEDICAL SUPPLY, THE	65, 91
ADA INJECTION	65
ADDOMS & GLOVER	56
ADOLHUS, DR. H.	65
AGUE KING	76
AH FUNG'S, DR.	80
ANIAXAB	26
ALFALFA CREAM	27
ALLEN'S	56, 66
ALLEN'S, MARTHA J.	65
AMARYLIS FOR THE COMPLEXION	31
ANGELL, FRANK B.	1
ANTIBILIOUS CURE	120
ARABALINE LOTION	26
ARCANUM	95
ARMSTRONG, C.W.	1
ARTHUR	1
ASPEN PHARMACY, THE	1
AUREOLINE	70
AUSTIN, F.A.	1
AUSTRALIAN BLOOD PURIFIER	107
BAILEY & EATON	66
BAKER, E.H.	2
BAKER, DR. IRA	66, 67, 131
BALDWIN, S.D., LINIMENT	67
BALDWIN'S DANDELION TONIC	67
BALDWIN PHARMACY	12
BALM OF MECCA	78
BALSAMIC CREAM OF ROSES	32
BARKER'S CELERY KOLA	67
BARNES, DR.	56, 57
BARNES' ALMOND CREAM	27
BARNES, CHRALES D., SNOW CREAM	27
BAUER, J.A.	35, 137
BEAR, BEN L.	2
BEARS GREASE	130
BENNET'S MAGIC CURE	67
BENSON, SMITH & CO.	25
BENTON'S, DR.J.B., LINIMENT	68
BENTE & CO., W.F.	2
BENZOATED WITCH HAZEL CREAM	29
BEST'S PHARMACY	2
BEUKMA, CORNELIUS	2
BIXBY'S SARSAPARILLA	131
BLISS LIVER & KIDNEY CURE	68
BLOOD POISON REMEDY	103
BLUMAUER, FRANK DRUG CO.	52
BOERICKE & TAFEL'S	68
BOGLE'S	68
BONE CO., THE W.H.	73
BORADENT CO., THE	27
BOSTON DRUG STORE	3, 137
BOTANIC COUGH BALSAM	123
BOTANIC PREPARATIONS	86
BOTHIN MANF'G CO.	57
BOUTHMAR'S, DR.	130
BOWEN'S, DR. BLOOD PURIFIER	69
BOWMAN & CO., H.	3
BOWMAN & SON	4
BOWMAN'S BEAUTIFUL SNOW	26
BOWMAN, H., DRUGGIST	3, 138
BOYCE, DR. J.R.	111
BOYSON'S PHARMACY	3
BRIGHTSBANE KIDNEY & LIVER CURE	68
BRIGHTON COLOGNE	43
BROADWAY PHARMACY, THE	2
BROEMMEL, B.	4
BRO. BENJAMIN'S HERBALO	68
BROWN PALACE HOTEL	17
BROWN'S, DR. COLLIS	57
BUCHARD'S, DR.	70
BUKER & COLSON	4
BURDELL'S TOOTH WASH	70, 129
BURK'S LIGHTNING LINIMENT	71
BURNETT & CO.	111
BURNETT, G.G.	4
BURTON'S FAMILY MEDICINES	70
BUTCHER DRUG CO., THE D.Y.	29
BUTTE TINE	70
CALIFORNIA CURE FOR ASTHMA	114
CALIFORNIA WASHING EXTRACT	35
CALIGARIS, J.	5, 71, 131
CALORIC VITA OIL	112
CAL. VOLCANIC MINERAL WATER CO.	72
CARSON RILEY DRUG CO.	5
CARY GUM TREE	72
C & B	40
C.C. LINIMENT	73
C.C.C. COUGH CURE	116
C., DR. E.	115
CELERY BEEF & IRON	87
CELRO KOLA	73
CENTRAL DRUG STORE	8
CHAMPLAIN'S, DR. E.	73
CHEATHAM'S	27
CHINESE REMEDY	83
CIRCASSIAN BLOOM	27
CITRATE OF MAGNESIA (only)	6
CITY DRUG STORE	7
CLARK, A.W.	6
CLARK'S, WM.A.	74
CLAYWORTH, J.C.	6
CLOSSON & KELLY	93
CLOVER LEAF CATARRH REMEDY	74
COFFIN & MAYHEW	6
COFFIN REDINGTON CO.	41
COLD CREAM	128, 129
COLE, A.M.	127, 152
COLE'S WHITE PINE STRUP	71
COLLINS, W.R., HAIR GROWER	49
COLORADO CREAM	29
COMPOUND EXTRACT OF MANZANITA	100
COMPOUND EXTRACT OF SARSAP.	131, 134, 135, 136
COMPOUND SYRUP EUCALYPTUS	71, 125
CONNELL'S	74
CONSOLIDATED DRUG CO.	16
COPPER'S, DR.	132
COPE'S, JOHN W.	75
CORAL HAIR RESTORATIVE	56
CORDIAL OF MOUNTAIN BALM	81
COUGH & CONSUMPTION CURE	119
COWAN & FLINT'S	76
CRANE & BRIGHAM	40, 57, 58, 95, 131
CRÈME DE LA CAMELIA	27
CRÈME DE LA CRÈME	30
CREWS BEGGS CO.	29
CROCKETT'S AMYGDALINE	75
CROCKWELL & SON, DR.	35
CROWELL, CRANE & BRIGHAM	132
CROWN OF SCIENCE	54
CUNNINGHAM, S.D.	7
CUNNINGWORTH, J.B.	137
CURLISS, DR., RHUEMATIC REMEDY	76
CURTIS COUGH CURE	76
DAMASCUS	29
DANDELION TONIC	87, 117
DAVID, B.B.	7
DAVIS BRO'S	41
D.D.D.	76
D.D.T.	90, 91
DEBECO REMEDIES	77
DE COCHEU	44
DERMAL CREAM	31
DICKEY PIONEER CHEMIST	28
DIGNAN, M.H., CHEMIST	35
DIPTHERIA REMEDY	82, 100
DOHERTY, J.	137

I

DOUBLE CONCENTRATED EXTRACTS	36
DRS. DARRIN	77
DRY CLIMATE CREAM	29, 30
DYSENTARY & DIARRHOREA CORDIAL	89
EAST INDIAN REMEDIES	74
EASTMAN & CO., J.D.	77
EDDY & CO.	8
E.H.R.	51
ELECTRIC LIFE	96, 97
ELECTRICITY IN A BOTTLE	124
ELECTRO MAGNETIC PHYSICIANS	77
ELECTRIC PAIN EXPELLER	92
ELIXIR FOR THE SKIN	26
ELLIOTT, H.A.	139
ELLIS, DOCTOR	77
ELY'S WILD CHERRY PHOSPHATE	77
EMULSION COD LIVER OIL	67
ENQUIST, A.A.	35
ETHEREAL COUGH SYRUP	89
EUREKA HAIR RESTORATIVE	49
F & CO.	79
FAIRHAVEN PHARMACY	7
FAIR'S PNEUMONIA MIXTURE	77
FAMILY LINIMENT	66
FARMER'S HEALING LINIMENT	79
FARMER'S HORSE MEDICINE	78
FARQUAR'S MEDICATED WINE	77
FEMALE RESTORATIVE	65
FEVER & AGUE MIXTURE	108
F.F.F.	78
FIRE OF LIFE	111, 122
FISH, B.F.	51
FISH'S INFALLIBLE HAIR RESTORATIVE	50
FIVE STAR LINIMENT	116
FLETCHER, DAVID M.	7
FLINT & CRANE	7, 8
FLINT'S, DR.A.E.	80
FOLGER & CO., J.A.	58
FORBES & CO., I.	51
FORCE'S ASTA MANNA	80
FORD, E.F.	8
FOUNTAIN OF YOUTH	49
FRESE, E.	58
FRESE'S EXTRACTS	36
FRIZELLE BROS.	36
FROST, JAMES	8
FRY'S	80, 132
FULTON'S RADICAL REMEDY	81
FURBER'S, DR.	81
GALLINGER'S & AULT	29
GARLAND'S COUGH DROPS	81
GATES	36
GATES, J.R. & CO.	57, 75, 84, 86, 132
GATES, JUSTIN	95
GERMAN ELIXIR	94
GERMAN INVIGORATOR	97
GIANT MEDICINE CO.	101, 135
GIRARDIN & CO., A.J.	26
GODBE & CO'S	58
GOLDEN BALSAM	110
GOLDEN GATE MEDICAL SYRUP	82
GOLDSTEIN'S. WM.	41
GOGINGS	81, 82, 138
GRAHAM & FISH	79
GRATTAN, DR. C.	82
GRAY HAIR RESTORER	52
GREAT CHINESE REMEDY	80
GREAT ELECTRIC HAIR TONIC	53
GREAT HAIR PRODUCER	54
GREENLEAF, T.A.	9
GREENMAN, ALFRED A.	9
GREEN'S LUNG RESTORER	83
GRIMM'S, A.	51
GUITTARD & CO.	36
GUM TREE	72
GUN OIL	66
GUN WA'S	83
GUPTILL'S SURE CURE	82
GUTMANN'S	29, 30
H.A. PERFUME CO.	42
HALL & CO., R.	56, 75
HALL'S	59, 132, 133
HALL'S HEPATIC KING	84
HALL'S PULMONARY BALSAM	84
HASSMER'S, VALENTINE	84
HASWELL'S WITCH HAZEL CREAM	84
HATCH, G.F.	9
HATHAWAY & CO., B.R.	85
HAVE'S, LEON	84
HAY, R.R.	139
HEADACHE & LIVER CURE	119
HELPING HAND	79
HENLEY'S	52
HENLEY'S, DOCTOR	87
HENLEY'S, DR.	52, 87, 88
HENRY'S, DR.	86, 133
HEPATIC KING	86
HERBALO FOR THE BLOOD	68
HERBS OF LIFE	86
HESPERIAN CHEMICAL ASSO.	37
HEUSSY DRUG CO.	11
HEUSSY & FILZ	9
H, G.W.	84
HICKORY BARK COUGH REMEDY	85
HILBY, F.M.	9, 36
HILL & CO., F.J.	10
HILLER'S, DR.	86
HILMER'S	89
HINCKLEY & CO., C.E.	10
HOARHOUND & ELECAMPANE	98
HOGAN, DR. J.J.	10
HOLDEN'S	89
HONDURAS CO'S	131
HOP CEL CO.	89
HORN, DR. JEROME	89
HORNUNG DRUG STORE, THE	10
HORSE LINIMENT	74, 103
HORSE MEDICINE	78, 90, 91
HORSNYDER, J.H.	10
HOSTETTER'S	59
HUG'S EXTRACTS	39
HUNT, D.D.	11
HURLBUT BROTHERS	59
IMPERIAL EMBROCATION	91
INDIAN BALM	106
INDIAN COUGH SYRUP	91
INDIAN QUEEN	52
INDIAN SARSAPARILLA	135
INDIAN TOO-REE	107
INDIAN TRA-QILLAUGH'S	106
INDIAN WIGWAM REMEDIES	91
INFALLIBALE INJECTION	116
INJECTION RECORD	110
ITALIAN REMEDY	106
IXL FLORIDA WATER	41
JAFFE'S	92
JAPANESE REMEDY	92
JOHNSON, C.E.	32
JOHNSON'S, W.M.	92
JONES, T.	52
JOY'S	93, 133
JOY'S PHARMACY	27
KAISER'S, DR.	94
KEATING & BABB	139
KEITH & CO., WM.H.	11, 140
KELLER BOHMANSSON DRUG CO.	11
KELLY, H.T.	139
KELLY'S, DR.	93
KETCHAM'S COUGH SYRUP	93
KING OF PAIN	99
KRONBERGER'S GREEN LIQUID	93
LAMB, AL.S.	12
LAMEROUX'S, DR.	95, 131
LANGENBACH'S DYSENTARY CURE	94
LANGLEY & CO., C.	37, 60, 134
LANGLEY & MICHAELS	42, 60
LAST CHANCE LINIMENT	108
L. DI. N.	42

II

Name	Pages
LECHNER'S, DR.	95
LEFEVRE, B.	127, 140, 152
LENGFELD, A.L.	12, 13
LEPPER'S, DR.	95, 96, 97
LEVI & CO., H.	37
LEVING'S	98, 135
LEWIS & CO., G.R.	13
LIEBIG'S, DR.	97
LIGNEOUS EXTRACT	73
LIGHTNING LINIMENT	71
LIPMAN, J.R.	51
LIVER REGULATOR	119
LORYEA & CO., DR.A.M.	98
LORD, F.J.	13
LOW'S EXTRACT	38
LULL'S ANTISPASMODOC	98
LUNG & COUGH SYRUP	84
LUXOR HAIR STIMULATOR	52
LYONS & CO., E.G.	60
MACK & CO., J.J.	38, 76, 80, 135
MACK'S BRIGHTON COLOGNE	43
MACK'S FLORIDA WATER	41
MAGIC COUGH CURE	122
MAGIG COUGH SYRUP	112
MARCHAND'S, MME.	30
MARVELOUS TONIC	123
MATHEW'S, DR.	52
MAYHEW & WENZELL	30
McBOYLE, A.M.	99, 109
McBRIDE, DR.J.J.	99
McCLELLAN'S	100
McCOMAS, H.	141
McDONALD & LEVY, DRS.	100
McDONNELL, JAS.	13
McFARLAND'S	30
McKENZIE BROS.	13
McLEAN'S, DR.E.E.	53
McMILLAN, DONALD	62
McMILLAN & KESTER	61
McCORMICK'S, J.A.	53, 70
MERTEN MFG. CO.	60
MERTEN MOFFIT & CO.	43, 61
MEYER'S COUGH REMEDY	101
MEYER'S SARSAPARILLA	135
MIKADO TONIC, THE	92
MILLER & WHITNEY'S	136
MINTIE'S DR.	101
MITCHELL'S	14, 61
MmcDELISDINERE	30
MONROE & CO., D.E.	30
MOON, JESSE H.	103
MOONPLANT	74
MOORE, WM.	14
MOORE'S REMEDY	101
MOREHEAD, G.A.	14
MORRILL, GEO. P.	37
MOTT'S, DR.	102
MOUNTAIN PILLS	124
MOUNTAIN TEA	97
MT. SHASTA KIDNEY CURE	75
MURRAY'S, DR. MAGIC CURE	102
N & N CHEM. CO.	65
NATIONAL HORSE LINIMENT	103
NELSON'S	104
NEPHRETICUM	101
NEUROTINE MANUFACTURING CO.	103
NEWELL'S PULMONARY SYRUP	103
NICHOL'S INJECTION	102
NICOLAI'S PHARMACY	15
NONE GENUINE	104
NORWEGIAN COD LIVER OIL	71
NOXON, DR.A.M.	104
ODONTO	129
O.G.W.	62
OIL OF GLADNESS	95
OREGON BLOOD PURIFIER	104
OREGON KIDNEY TEA	105
OVERLAND LINIMENT	112
PACIFIC GLASS WORKS	105
PACIFIC PHARMACY	15
PAIN EXPELLER	92
PALA VERDE BALSAM	105
PALMER, S.A.	15
PALMETTO OIL	95
PARADISE OIL	106
PAREIRA'S, DR.	106
PARKER, DR. R.	106
PARKINSON, W.S.	15
PATTERSON'S PHARMACY	15
PAWNEE	106, 107
PAXSON'S DERMALA	31
PEARL ROSE CREAM	27
PEARSE & MCGILL	15
PECTORAL BALSAM	66
PERFECTION FLORIDA WATER	42
PERRY'S, DR.	108
PETER'S, C.J.	38
PETIBEAU & CO., E.	141
PETTI'S, DR.	107
PFEISTER, CHRETEIN	108
PFUNDER & CO., W.	16, 104, 108, 155
PHILICOME	130
PIONEER 1850	31
PIXLEY, W.B.	141
PLOUF'S, DR.	109
POLLARD, C.P.	139
POND, HIRAM	16, 135
POND'S	110
POPULAR REMEDY	89
PORTER'S SARSAPARILLA	135
POWER'S, A.H.	102
P.P.M. CO.	105
PRAIRIE FLOWER	125
PRATT'S ABOLITION OIL	99, 109
PRATT'S NEW LIFE	99, 109
PURE HERB TONIC	92
QUAKER BALM	68
QUAKER DRUG CO., THE	16
RADICAL REMEDY	81
RAGSDALE & CO., MRS.	53
RATTLER OIL	124
RAWLINS DRUG CO.	16
REAVES, M.A.	53
RED CROSS PHARMACY	16
REDINGTON & CO.	44, 45, 62, 103
REDINGTON'S	38
REGULATOR	88
REILLY, P.J.	49
REJUVENATOR FOR THE HAIR	51
RHEUMATIC REMEDY	76
RHODES & CO.	39
RHODES & TROXELL	16
RICHARD'S	110
RIEGER'S, PAUL	38, 62
ROBERTINE	34
ROBERTS & CO., B.F.	82
ROBINSON, L.P.	31
ROSES & ROSEMARY, EXTRACT OF	104
ROWELL'S, DR.	111
ROWLER'S	111
ROYAL BALSAM	88
RUBEL & BOULTON	17
S. & CO. BLOOD PURIFIER	112
SAMSON, W.R.	17
SANDELIN, FRED	111
SAPONACEOUS TOOTH POWDER	128
SARSAPARILLA & ROSE WILLOW	135
SCHMIDT & BRO. H.W.	130
SCHOENHEIT, A.	117
SCHOPPE, A.	17
SCOTT, J.B.	17, 112, 142
SEARBY'S	46
SHATTUCK'S FAMILY MEDICINES	117
SHAW, B.F.	17
SHAW, FRED C.	17
SHAW'S GLYCERINE LOTION	31, 112
SHEPARDSON & GATES	57, 133

SHERRY & IRON CO., THE	113
SIGNORETT'S, DR.	135, 136
SILVER STATE	112
SKIDMORE, S.G.	18
SKINNER & CO., R.W.	18
SMITH BROS.	98
SMITH & CO., A.H.	18, 31
SMITH & DAVIS	18, 39, 155
SMITH, C.E.	19
SMITH, DR. BARLOW J.	112
SMITH, W.H.	18
SNAKE ROOT OIL LINIMENT	91
SNOW'S VICTORY, JOHN F.	113
SPENCE, E.F.	141
SPIEKER, J.J.	39
SPOONHAUER'S, M.	113
SPRUANCE, STANLEY & CO.	102
SQUARZA, V.	114
STARK'S CATARRAH INHALENT	113
ST. CLAIR'S HAIR LOTION	54
STEELE & CO., J.G.	19, 46
STEWART, A.B.	116, 117, 135, 136
STEWART & HOLMES	19, 20, 1136, 136
STOCKTON DRUG CO.	20
STODDART BROS.	29
STRATENA	84
STREAMERS COUGH SYRUP	115
STREAMER, F.M.	20
STREAMER & WHITNEY	20
STRONG, W.R.	115
SUCH'S	114
SUN DRUG CO.	115
SWEET'S LIVER CLEANSER, DR.	85
SYRUP OF FIGS	110, 115
TALLMAN, L.L.	20
TEMPLE OF HEALTH	117
THAT WONDEROUS LINIMENT	117
THAXTER, C.C.	152
THAYER & CO., B.B.	39, 128
THE SPECIFIC SELF CURE	113
THOMPSON'S	117
TILTON, PROF. J.R.	54
TIP TOP COUGH SYRUP	117
TODD'S PHARMACY	124
TOIYABE CHOLERA REMEDY	118
TOPLEY, JAMES	20
TRAUTZ, OTTO	21
TRIB A LINIMENT	118
TRITURATIONS	68
TROUT OIL LINIMENT	120
TRUNK BROS.	21, 118
TRUNK, ED. F.	21
TURNER'S	63, 119
TUTTLE, CHAS. K.	21
TWIABA	55
UMATILLA INDIAN RELIEF	118
UNEMBOSSED	64
UNIVERSITY DRUG STORE, THE	21, 142
UNKWEED REMEDY	98
U-R-DAS	31
URSINA	129
VALLEY TAN REMEDIES	32
VAN DYKE'S, DR.	120
VANDENBERGH'S, DR. J.P.P.	121
VANDENBERGH'S SR., DR. S.P.P.	121
VANDERPOOL'S, DR.	119
VERMIN DESTROYER	119
VIAVI CO, THE	122
VIGOR OF LIFE	121
VINCENT'S, DR. D.B.	122
W	64
WAIT'S	123
WAKELEE & CO.,	22, 23, 70, 104, 129, 130, 142
WAKELEE'S CAMELLINE	33
WAKELEE'S PHARMACIES	23
WARREN'S, DR.	123
WATSON'S LING BALSAM, DR.	124
WEB'S	123
WELCH'S, DR.	124
WELLS & CO., C.H.	24
W.E.M.	46, 48
WENZELL, W.T.	63
WEST ELECTRIC CURE CO.	124
WESTERN PERFUMERY CO.	47
WHITE & CO., R.E.	23
WHITE ROSE CREAM	30
WHITE'S	125
WHITNEY BLAKE PHARMACY	24
WHITNEY'S SARSAPARILLA	136
WILD CHERRY TONIC	102, 123
WILHELM, C.L.	25
WILLIAM'S, DR. H.	124
WILLIAMS'	32
WINDSOR PHARMACY	24
WISDOM'S	24, 34
WITCH HAZEL CREAM	84
WONDERFUL GERMAN INVIGORATOR	97
WOOD, W.H.	142
WOODWARD, CLARKE & CO.	24, 31, 33, 132
WORM SYRUP	120
WORNER'S	124
WRIGHT & BROWN	39
WYNKOOP VAUGHN CO.	24
YELLOW DOCK	132
YERBA SANTA	126
ZAMBALDANO, DR. A.	125
ZELLE, CARL	130